With my highest compliment.
Your brother in christ
William Ekane
2/2/2023

One Flesh:
The Winning Team

A PRACTICAL GUIDE TO A HAPPY, HEALTHY, AND LASTING MARRIAGE

Dr. William Ekane

Published by Kingdom View Press

ISBN: 978-0-9988408-0-2 (Print)
ISBN: 978-0-9988408-0-2 (Digital)
Library of congress Control Number – 2017908909

While the stories in this book are true, some names and identifying information may have been changed to protect the privacy of those mentioned.

Interior Layout by Penoaks Publishing, http://penoaks.com

CONTENTS

ACKNOWLEDGMENTS

With deepest appreciation to:

- Samuel Ekane, whose tireless efforts and editorial skills have made this book possible.
- Francis Ikome, for his help in typing portions of the manuscript.
- Joshua Ekane, Carl Johnson, and Dr. Julius Monangai, for their editing and insightful suggestions.
- Friends and family, whose marriages serve as a guiding pillar for this book.
- A special thanks to the dynamic members of New Life Fellowship Global Ministries.
- Lastly, to you the reader, I am honored that you've taken the time to read "One Flesh: The Winning Team". The purpose of this book is to build your marriage on a solid foundation so that the love you have for your spouse will never be extinguished.

Part 1: The Creation of the Universe

"If life is an accident, it cannot conceivably have any purpose, for accident and purpose are mutually exclusive."

– JOHN BLANCHARD

Do you ever ponder how the universe came into existence? What are the essential components of the cosmos? These questions are fundamental to understanding the genesis of life – living and non-living things – man, the family, and other societal institutions.

There is a consensus in the scientific community – whether you subscribe to the Big Bang Theory or hold to a Biblical worldview – that the universe consists of three essential elements: time, space, and matter. However, there are two divergent views as to the source of the cosmos; evolutionism and the creationism. The evolutionists hold a view that the cosmos was created in a massive explosion that not only created the majority of matter, but also the physical laws that govern our ever-expanding galaxy. This, they call the Big Bang Theory. Many reputable scientists have posed questions regarding this philosophy that have yet to be answered. For instance, how do we know that our universe was conceived in a massive explosion? What proof supports this theory? What does the theory say about the long-term projections for our universe? On the other hand, creationists who adhere to the intelligent design model believe that a supernatural intelligence was behind the creation of the universe. Their Biblically based worldview states that God is the creator of all things. He created everything that is visible (and invisible) out of nothing by the power of His Word, and equally sustains everything with this same power.[1] Their argument is simple and straightforward – every created thing has a designer. For example, a watch doesn't just appear from nothing, it was made by a watchmaker. Likewise, cars do not fall from the sky and houses do not grow from the soil. These tools are manufactured. So too the universe didn't come into existence by chance: there must be an intelligent designer.

God, in his infinite knowledge, realized that when He created Adam from the dust, he would be lonely. As a result, He created Eve. Together, Adam and Eve exemplified God's plan and formed the concept that we now know as the family unit. By presenting biblical insights and godly principles, this book will help you truly understand and apply God's truth in a covenant marriage. You will also learn the needs of engaged couples, newlyweds, and the not-so-newlyweds. In other words, whether you've been married for a long time, recently tied the knot, or are considering getting married, you will gain valuable insights on the *essential* building blocks to ensuring a loving, thriving, and lasting relationship.

From the foundations of the Earth, the family has been God's core unit upon which He built all other institutions of society. The Psalmist David declares, "Of old You laid the foundations of the Earth, and the Heavens are the works of Your hands."[2] The family is God's idea; indeed, it is His primary idea. Civil government and the church also come from the mind of God. Prior to this, even before He created these institutions, God thought of the family first. As stated earlier, from the very beginning He looked at Adam and said it is not good for man to be alone.[3]

Marriage, per God's design, is about helping couples grow closer to each other and closer to God. It is about knowing and loving each other, while knowing and loving God. The resources needed for a healthy, happy, and thriving relationship are the same ones we need for everyday living – love, joy, peace, patience, kindness, goodness, faithfulness, gentleness, and self-control. These divine virtues, found in the Bible, are called the fruit of the Spirit. As we grow in our walk with God through Jesus Christ, exercising these Spiritual gifts, our marital relationships grow as well.

With the breakdown of marriage comes the deterioration of family life. Sadly, those who suffer most are the children. For many, they are cut adrift spiritually and are left at the mercy of societal influence, which normally steers them away from the path of following God. When spiritual leadership is missing, the defenses around the family are shattered, leaving children vulnerable to all sorts of influences.

As stated earlier, the family is the building block of society. So as the family unit deteriorates, our society suffers. This cascading effect can be fixed by applying fundamental Biblical principles to relationships, beginning with the head of the home. It is significant to note that although man is appointed head of the home, he's not qualitatively superior to the woman. After all, God the Father outranks God the Holy Spirit in the Godhead, but it would be wrong to state that the Father is qualitatively "better" than the Holy Spirit or Christ. Indeed, they are one. It is simply a matter of spiritual ranking and responsibility. In like manner, the headship of a man over a woman does not mean that the husband owns his wife or is superior to her.

In God's economy, the Father is the head of Christ, and Christ is the head of the Church. Christ is also the head of man. The husband is head of his wife, and both parents are head over their children. Just as there is no schism between the Father and His Son, so should there be no schism between a man and his wife. This truth makes sure that the husband looks up to Christ for leadership at home.

The Biblical perspective points to the Creator – God. Moses outlines how each of these elements (time, space, and matter) came about.[4] He states, "In the beginning", which represents time; "God created the heavens" which stands for space; and "and the Earth" depicts matter. Thus, the Biblical account is consistent with the elements that constitute the cosmos. God, who is as infinite as the universe and as enduring as eternity, created the worlds as they now exist. However, He lives outside of time, space, and matter. In other words, God cannot be contained in what He created – He transcends all elements of the cosmos.

According to the creation account in Genesis, God has set in motion a graduated order of creation. God Himself is over all as Lord of lords, King of kings, eternal, infinite, and omnipotent. Below Him is the angelic order – magnificent beings of light and glory. Below them are humans, whom God created "a little lower than angels".[5] He has placed us on Earth to tend and exercise dominion over plants and animals. Per the Scriptures, Jesus Christ came down to our planet to redeem mankind. Though He was Himself God, He became human; the God-man was made a little lower than the angels in order to die for mankind.

Paul instructs, "In your relationships with one another, have the same mindset as Christ Jesus: Who, being in very nature God, did not consider equality with God something to be used to his own advantage; rather, he made himself nothing by taking the very nature of a servant, being made in human likeness."[6]

Jesus became man for men, to save mankind from sin's penalty and justly grant us eternal life. Following His resurrection, He ascended back to heaven to resume the glory He had with the Father before the world began. "Therefore, God also has highly exalted Him and given Him the name which is above every name... in heaven... and on Earth."[7] The Bible teaches that there are three heavens: the atmospheric (the air and space surrounding our immediate atmosphere), the stellar heavens (the sun, moon, and stars), and the third heaven, which is the home of God.

In the Genesis account, we are told that God created man in His own image. "Then God said, 'Let us make mankind in our image, in our likeness, so that they may rule over the fish in the sea and the birds in the sky, over the livestock and all the wild animals, and over all the creatures that move along the ground.' So God created mankind in his own image, in the image of God he created them; male and female he created them."[8] God created Adam first, "Then the Lord God formed a man from the dust of the ground and breathed into his nostrils the breath of life, and the man became a living being."[9] The narrative also unveils that the Lord planted a garden where man was put to manage God's affairs. Later, God solved the problem of man's loneliness by creating a helpmate – Eve. "So the Lord God caused the man to fall into a deep sleep; and while he was sleeping, He took one of the man's ribs and then closed up the place with flesh. Then the Lord God made a woman from the rib He had taken out of the man, and He brought her to the man. The man said, 'This is now bone of my bones and flesh of my flesh; she shall be called 'woman,' for she was taken out of man.'"[10]

In summary, Jehovah Elohim (Creator) conceived the idea of marriage and family. Genesis chapter 2 details the creation of marriage and family. There are several reasons marriage was created. These include: company, pleasure, procreation, and for man to exercise delegated authority over God's handiwork. In the beginning of Genesis 3, Satan comes in to deceive man and woman, derailing them from God's beautiful plan. Later, in the Genesis account, we see how Cain killed his brother Abel. As witnessed here, Satan's strategy has always been to steal, kill, and destroy.[11] His ultimate purpose is to unhinge the foundations of the family. The Psalmist says, "When the foundations are being destroyed, what can the righteous do?"[12] The word "foundation" in this verse is a transliteration of the word 'purpose' or 'plan'. The foundations here do not represent the foundations of a house. The author's intent is to convey the idea of the destruction of God's first institution – the family. Today, the enemy is doing everything in his power to destroy God's purpose and plan for the family. However, he won't succeed because God equips believers with the Holy Spirit who resides in them to accomplish His task of rebuilding the family. Presently, Satan is attacking the very foundations of our society by breaking up families through:

- illegal relationships – people living together without a commitment to themselves or to God's institution of marriage
- homosexuality – redefining marriage between a man and woman to people of the same sex
- divorce – permanent separation made easy
- abortion – destruction of human life
- polygamy – having many spouses at one time

Against this backdrop, the question we need to ask ourselves is: what must *we* the righteous do? We must implement God's blueprint to build the family structure as He originally intended it to be. In the next piece, titled "Is God your Father?", you will be introduced to the true God and learn how to have a personal relationship with Him. The main text of this book covers these topics:

- Chapter 1 presents God's principles for choosing your life partner.
- Chapter 2 discusses living and cleaving with your partner.
- Chapter 3 describes how the couple must see each other from God's perspective.
- Chapter 4 focuses on communication in a covenant relationship.
- Chapter 5 presents God's financial management blueprint.
- Chapter 6 describes intimacy in marriage.
- Chapter 7 talks about the building blocks of building a winning team using the win-Win-win paradigm.

Reflections on Creation of the Universe

- Does the biblical perspective of the cosmos have more credence than the narrative of the evolutionist perspective?
- If your perspective is biblical, what Scripture verse can you cite to support your position?
- What role are you going to play in enforcing God's directives, according to Psalm 11:3?

Part 2: Is God Your Father?

"It is when people forget God, that tyrants forge their chains."

– PATRICK HENRY

God the Father

Scriptures speak of three fathers: God the Father, Adam our first human father, and Satan. God the Father created both Adam and Satan. According to the Bible, Yahweh is revealed as self-existing, self-determining, self-sufficient, immutable, holy, omnipotent, omniscient, omnipresent, omnibenevolent (all loving), and eternal, possessing life in Himself. As a benevolent Father, He designed mankind to have a personal relationship with Him. That's why He created man in His own image. He isn't just well acquainted with our physical being, but also knows our actions and thoughts even before we speak. Each step we take is known by Him; there is nowhere we can go that is out of His sight or reach. The Psalmist declares that God not only knows us as individuals, but lays His hand upon us and "hems" us in from behind and before.

The word "hem" means to protect. He takes on the role as our protector since our future lies squarely in His hands. God promises an incredible life for each of His children. With open hands and a watchful eye, His ears are open to all who call upon Him in spirit and in truth. You are safe and secure today, tomorrow, and for all eternity. His Word declares, "For I know the plans I have for you... plans for good and not for evil, to give you a future and a hope. And in those days when you pray [or call on Me] I will listen."[1]

What was topmost on God's mind before He created the world? Not angels, not the cosmos, not heaven or Earth, or anything visible or invisible – but man. Paul, writing to the Ephesians said, "Even before He made the world, God loved us and chose us in Christ to be holy and without fault in His eyes. God decided in advance to adopt us into His own family by bringing us to Himself through Jesus Christ. This is what He wanted to do, and it gave Him great pleasure."[2] Let's be clear, mankind was on God's mind first because He wanted a family. From the above verses, it's evident that God planned to adopt us even though He knew we would fail Him as recorded in Genesis. His strategy was to send Jesus to rescue mankind, a plan that culminated at the cross.

Adam

Adam, our first father, was designed by our heavenly Father. The Scriptures reveal that all families of the Earth came into being through Adam and Eve. When God created our first parents, He gave them the ability to think and choose. God placed them in the Garden of Eden, a perfect environment, and put them in charge of every created thing. He also commanded them not to eat from the tree of knowledge of good and evil. Then came Satan, who offered them a tempting proposition – to be like God, knowing good and evil. The reader sees that Adam and Eve have a clear choice – to listen to God's directives or heed Satan's deception. God desired their love, but did not demand it. Their choice, evidently, had far-reaching consequences that are seen in our society today. They chose to eat the fruit of the tree of knowledge and instantly realized the consequences of their actions. We are offered the same choice today. Because of Adam and Eve's choice, Paul reminds us that we are born with an inclination to sin.[3] David the Psalmist confirms that he was born in iniquity, and so are we.[4] Thankfully, because of God's love for us, He sent His Son to die for us while we were still in our sin. Now through Christ Jesus, we can choose life and obedience.

Satan

As indicated earlier, Satan is a created cherub. He was originally designed to cover the very throne of God. He was created perfect and blameless, full of wisdom and beauty. His *pride* lifted his sense of self-worth and inflated his ego, making him unrighteous before the eyes of God.[5] He was created as the highest ranked of all created beings, greater than angel Michael and angel Gabriel in both size and power. However, Satan's pride caused his downfall. On his descent, he convinced one-third of the angels to rebel with him against God and His plan for humanity. The Scriptures reveal several of his names:

- god of this world[6]
- angel of light[7]
- prince of the power of the air[8]
- lawless one[9]
- dragon, ancient serpent, The Devil, and Satan[10]

Most remarkable of all, Jesus calls Him "father of lies".[11] He now deceives the whole world, as he did to Adam and Eve, and the "whole world lies under his power".[12] We are given the same choice today: to choose God or Satan as our spiritual father. It is incumbent upon us not to make the same choice that Adam and Eve made. When we choose God as Father, we automatically become a part of His family. As family members, we will enjoy eternity with Him. No amount of religious activity and experience (i.e., church attendance, membership enrollment, good works, self-sacrifice, baptism, etc.) will pay the debt of sin that we owe God. Our freedom to choose does not guarantee that we will make wise decisions or escape the consequences of our foolish acts. Only through the sacrificial death, burial, and resurrection of Jesus Christ can we find freedom from the penalties of sin, guilt, and hell. Although the cost of our salvation was enormous, Jesus gladly paid the price for us and purchased us with His own blood.[13] We are chosen, we are redeemed, and we are greatly loved by the Father. When we choose to become members of God's family, we are automatically co-heirs with Christ, and our status changes from debtor to inheritor.[14] It is worth noting that salvation is received by faith alone, through Christ alone. Like Paul, the life we now live in the flesh, we live by faith in the Son of God who loves us and gave Himself for us. You may be asking, what must I do? Speak out the following faith statements:

1. I realize, after reading the above, that I am a sinner in need of a Savior.
2. I believe that Jesus died on the cross in my place.
3. I know that He is the only one who can save me from my sin debt.
4. I willingly confess my sins and ask for God's forgiveness through Jesus Christ.
5. I trust that with God's help, I will live the life He intended for me.
6. I thank God, through Jesus, for saving me, and I will continue to seek the Spirit's help every day of my life.

Now say this prayer: "Thank you Lord, for sending your Son Jesus Christ to die on my behalf. Thank you for making me a member of the family of God. In Jesus' name. Amen"

Your Assurance

- God has chosen you and has a plan for your life.[15]
- God is patient with you even when you commit acts of unrighteousness.[16]
- God desires to transform you into the likeness of His Son Jesus Christ.[17]
- God will never leave you or forsake you, He remains faithful.[18]

CHAPTER 1

Choosing the Love of Your Life

"The righteous chooses his friends carefully."

(PROVERBS 12:26)

Below are 5 examples of real, happily married Christian couples, counseled by my wife and me. We pray that your true love story is as vivid and as beautiful as these:

1. Ruth and Emmanuel

God makes all things beautiful in His time: Emmanuel and Ruth's love story is simply a manifestation of God's work. They knew each other from childhood since their parents were friends. Nobody knew this couple would end up binding the two families together – "till death do us part". Growing up, they attended each other's birthday parties and other social activities together. Their parents, particularly their mothers, were prayer partners along with other women of faith. These women laid their hearts before God, asking for direction in many areas of their lives concerning the present and future needs of their families. They prayed that their children would end up in Christ-centered, loving relationships. Little did they know how these prayers would be answered. While they both attended college, Emmanuel left Oklahoma to attend a Christian conference in Atlanta where Ruth was invited to sing. Being reunited after over 15 years, Emmanuel realized he saw something in Ruth that he needed: a partner to help him fulfill his mission on Earth. After two weeks of celebrating life with mutual friends and family in Atlanta, he approached Ruth and indicated his interest in starting a relationship. It didn't take long before she confirmed that her heart was at peace with giving it a try. Within a month, they were both convinced that their relationship was God-ordained. After over seven years of marriage and two kids, the feeling is still mutual.

2. *Tamara and Caleb*

"It all began at The University at North Georgia. One day, when I was walking to my military leadership class, I saw "the Hackett twins" for the first time. As I proceeded to class I saw Tammy and her sister acting in the capacity of a drill instructor, grilling some poor soul about something he did wrong. He was definitely wilting under the intense pressure they were placing on him. I made a mental note to stay away from those two so I wouldn't meet the same fate. Although

Tammy was a stunning beauty, her harsh tone towards the poor sap drove me away from talking to her at that time. Despite that first impression, we met and maintained a casual friendship with short conversations. We both eventually graduated and went our separate ways. Tammy relocated to New York to work in the marketing industry while I moved to Phoenix City, Alabama to work at Fort Benning. After a few years apart, Tammy moved back to Georgia and we decided to catch up on old times. Speaking to her, I realized that I completely misjudged Tammy from when we first met and I became quite enamored with her. After a couple of months, we decided to date exclusively. Over time we found out just how much we complement each other and that we share many of the same interests. I was searching for a God-fearing woman with a good sense of humor and a keen business acumen, and God gave me my perfect match: a woman who embodies these attributes and more. I thank God for her, my daily reminder of the long-lost rib taken from my side. Marriage is a give and take relationship, best viewed as a triangle. God is at the top and the two married partners are at the opposite ends. The more the married partners dedicate themselves to God and divest themselves of their *wants*, the more the base of the triangle shrinks. As we apply this concept daily in our marriage, we bring ourselves closer to each other and become more selfless each day."

3. Louisa and Ivan

"As I write this, my wife Louisa and I have now been married for over 11 years, since August 5th, 2005. Our paths crossed for

the first time in September 1994 in BHS Buea, Cameroon. I
was a new student in the high school and she was one year
under me in form 5. I had come from CPC Bali, where our
Bible club had played a major part in my Christian experience
and my commitment to Christ. Saturday afternoon was a
devotional day and I decided to visit the gospel team/prayer
group in our area. After the meeting, I got to meet and greet
some of the students who were present – that's when I met
Louisa. I remember how vividly she stood out to me and I had
a witness in my heart, I believe from the Spirit of Christ,
saying: "She is going to be your wife one day". I tried to shy
away from the thought because I thought marriage was out of
place for my age. Over time, Louisa and I became fond of each
other and exchanged many letters. Our conversations centered
on encouraging each other in our faith in Christ Jesus. When
she graduated from high school, I hoped she would join me at
the University of Buea. I was sad when she told me that she
would attend another University in Dschang, in the western
Province of Cameroon. A year later, she travelled to the USA
to study for her Bachelor's degree. We lost touch for nearly
three years and I felt prompted to get back in touch with her
when I talked to one of her classmates. It felt like a breath of
fresh air when we got back in touch and more so when we
started exchanging emails for the first time. We had a long-
distance relationship for a season, but it was different because
we choose a day to fast and pray together. We talked about
everything. I went to graduate school in Germany in 2001, and
that same year she moved to the Netherland Antilles to begin
medical school. Prayer and extended phone conversations that

had lasted nearly 3 years were the sum of our dating experience. We felt like we knew each other and understood each other so well that when we met in Limavady, North Ireland in June 2003, after about 7 years of being physically apart, it did not feel like we had any gap in our communication. I prayerfully considered proposing to marry her for a period of time. I loved her and felt like God had a plan for both of us. On March 3rd, 2003, I asked her over the phone to prayerfully consider if she would like to be my partner for life. Her reply stunned me. I expected that she would take her time to give me a reply. She said she didn't need to pray about it anymore, because in fact she had been ready all along. She said YES! We were both so elated that we hardly slept that night. We chatted with expectation and joy about our future for endless hours. It was almost morning my time in Goettingen, Germany and midnight her time in St. Eustatius when we bade good night to each other. I went on my knees and asked her, again, to marry me when we met in June. On June 12, I gave her an engagement ring and promised to marry her in the presence of her mother. We prayed through the process. We planned to get married at the end of that year, but ran into logistical difficulties. God brought a dear father and Pastor, Dr. William Ekane into our lives. He was a family friend to Louisa's family and she lived with his family in Atlanta, GA at the time. I travelled to the USA in December 2004, and he took time to counsel with us. It gave us much needed preparation and helped us stay on a firm foundation to get married. Louisa had lost her father 3 years before, and in him I saw someone I could relate to as a father figure to Louisa. He [Dr. Ekane] set an outstanding model as a husband of 30 years, as well as a father of children who were within our age group. We were so blessed to have him and New Life Fellowship officiate our wedding on August 5th, 2005. In many ways, we have had a journey of faith, and have been a source of strength to each other before the Lord our God through the years. His answers to our prayers have been too numerous to recount here. She is still my best friend, and we are still happily married. We have been blessed with three beautiful children, Zoey, Praise, and Sophia who are nine, five, and one respectively. We built our home around the cross of Christ and nurture our children with the overflow of the love of Christ we have found, and the love we have for one another."

4. Cecile and Richard

"The first time I saw her was in October 1999 in Buea, Cameroon. The school year had just started at the University of Buea and she was a freshman. Back then, we had a close-knit group of friends, all students of UB and members of the CMFI church. It was a Saturday evening and we were celebrating a friend's birthday. She'd been invited by some mutual friends she'd known in high school. The first thing I noticed about her was how pretty, young, and soft spoken she was. The following day (Sunday) she came to our student body service, and to my surprise it was announced that she had a song. My first impression was "Why on Earth would they call this young lady to sing on her very first time here? What is she going to sing?" Then, she opened her mouth and everyone was stunned. I was the choir leader, and she eventually became a member of our student body and choir. If someone had even suggested that we would end up together, we would have probably thought that person was insane. We were not necessarily close, but we always kept a cordial relationship. She attended my college for just one academic year, and eventually relocated to the States. I would not see her again for about seven years until we met at the wedding of a mutual friend. What began as an occasional text or phone call between old friends catching up eventually morphed into a beautiful relationship. We recently celebrated nine years of our relationship, and will soon be celebrating six years of marriage with the bonus of a beautiful baby boy."

5. *Joy and Will*

Will and Joy met through a mutual friend. Will felt led to reach out to this friend, who recommended Joy to him after he described what he was looking for in a soulmate. Will thanked her, but informed her he would like to take some time to seek God's guidance before moving forward with contacting her. After a couple weeks of praying and seeking God's guidance on whether or not to reach out, Will got the confirmation he needed. Before asking Joy for her number, the mutual friend shared some information to Joy that confirmed Will was a believer. Furthermore, she answered the few questions Joy had about Will concerning his age and height. The main thing that got Joy's attention was the fact that he was a God-fearing man, volunteered in his church, was in the same line of work, and was spoken highly of by this mutual friend. When Will

contacted Joy for the first time, she was on her way to her
friend's baby shower. They spoke at length the next day – the
conversation flowed as if they had known each other for years.
Will made his intentions known – which was to have a long-
term relationship with a God-fearing woman who also shared
some of his interests. Besides their mutual love for God, they
soon realized that they had much in common: like the
structure of their respective families, their undergraduate
majors, and their lifestyles. Early into the relationship, Joy's
parents saw Will as a son, and her family embraced him
almost immediately. Similarly, Will's parents adopted Joy as a
daughter, and his family welcomed her with open arms. Six
months later, Will proposed at Joy's parents' home with the
family present. Nine months after the proposal, they tied the
knot in the presence of God, with both sets of parents,
families, and friends.

Marriages are made in heaven but are lived out on Earth.
They were conceived in God's mind, designed for His glory,
and serve as a blessing and benefit to his people.

Before believers start dating, they ought to seek God's will
for their union. A careful observation of God's instruction in
the Scriptures about marriage will help each prospective
couple strive to make their marriage flow according to His
plan. If they follow the Architect's design, not only will God

be pleased, but they will reap the fruit of a joyful and lasting relationship. It is significant to note that true fulfillment in a covenant relationship is not found in either partner, but in God.

Consulting self-help books, secular ideas, and philosophies do tremendous damage to individuals, the family unit, and society. This damage presents itself both intellectually and morally. Therefore, it's imperative that we turn to the Architect's design for the home and family. God's design for the home is the only genuine plan that provides for the best family relationships. It builds strong family units for the well-being of churches, communities, societies, and nations. So, the ideal for each prospective couple is to strive towards God's original plan for marriage. When God's plan is adhered to, He promises the family "long living" in the land. He also promises spiritual and moral well-being, prosperity, and great success. The home where God is honored and worshipped is the best environment on Earth, and is the closest place to Heaven where kids can be nurtured. Let your relationship with God become your source of marital fulfillment.

Five Major Warnings in Making Marital Choices:

Alternative Marriages

The Scriptures warn us against violating God's plan for marriage. Under no circumstances has God given the Christ-follower the luxury to redefine marriage. The believer has an obligation to reaffirm, not redefine, God's design of one man and one woman, because from the beginning God created us male and female. Paul confirms, "In God's plan, men and women need each other."[1] God created marriage for the connection of men and women. Malachi says, "She's your companion and your wife by covenant."[2] Nobody holds the full image of God; since men have a part and women have a part, we need each other. God the Architect wired it this way; God thought up gender, created sex, and formed what we know as the traditional marriage. In God's economy, He made man first and woman after. He wanted Adam to see his need for a companion. God says, "It isn't good for man to be alone, I will make a companion for him."[3] Although humans need other humans for relationships, the marriage companionship is in a relational class all by itself. Here's what Jesus said about marriage, "God made them male and female from the beginning of creation. This explains why a man leaves his father and mother and is joined to his wife, and the two are united into one. Since they are no longer two but one, let no one split apart what God has joined together."[4]

We can draw three major lessons from the text above:

1. *Marriage is God's plan* – It's not a tradition we can just ignore or redefine. We can see in our culture today that cultural pundits, political leaders, and judicial activists usurp God's authority and have redefined the terms of marriage, especially in some western societies. They make marriage all-inclusive, adding same-sex marriage to God's original plan. In other parts of the world, such as Africa, prearranged marriages are performed. Also,

in Asia and Africa, polygamous relationships are tolerated. In some western cultures, some partners agree that each is free to engage in extramarital sex – including group marriages, human-animal marriages, and open marriages – without regard to fidelity.

2. *Bonding* – In the beginning, God created the single man, and out of man he created woman. God's idea of marriage brings singularity where there was once a duality in human nature; He wants the two to become one.

3. *No Separation* – God has given clear instructions that no one has the right to separate what He has put together.

In 1960, the Atlantic reported that approximately 450,000 couples in America were living together outside of God's prescribed plan for marriage. In 2015, the New York Times announced that the number had increased to more than 7 million, a 900% increase in the last 55 years alone.[5] For newly engaged couples, there is great value in being informed about the benefits of honoring God's plan for your marriage. First, your bodies were designed for each other's sexual urges. God created us with powerful desires to guarantee the continuity of the human race. We must channel our desires in God's ways as He has directed. Second, a simple family home with a husband and wife is the best environment for raising children. Third, joining hearts with another for the sake of testimony and ministry is truly a powerful witness to a watching world. Priscilla and Aquila, in the book of Acts, are good examples.

They helped Paul and Apollos in their ministry. They did not only support Paul, they explained the gospel perfectly to Apollos, the great orator. Therefore, plan to live according to His plan, and determine to build your home according to His design.

Getting Married to an Unbeliever

A second caveat is getting married to an unbeliever. God desires marriages to be loving and lasting, between one man and one woman in a monogamous relationship. However, the relationship must be between a husband and wife who are both children of God. This mirrors the relationship between Christ and His Church. Listen to Paul's strict admonition, "Don't team up with those who are unbelievers. How can righteousness be a partner with wickedness? How can light live with darkness? What harmony can there be between Christ and the devil? How can a believer be a partner with an unbeliever? And what union can there be between God's temple and idols? For we are the temple of the living God. As God said: 'I will live in them and walk among them I will be their God and they will be my people.'"[6] From the text, we glean two fundamental principles to abide by. First, every genuinely twice-born child of God has the presence of the Holy Spirit in them at the moment of conversion. It is the Spirit of God that sets them apart as good, as being in the light, and as God's temples. The unbeliever, on the other hand, is controlled by his fleshly human nature that is described as wicked. He lives in darkness and does not possess God's Spirit in Him. Second, because God lives in the believer, he or she can't live and walk in fellowship with an unbeliever. The believer has God as their Father, while unbelievers have the Devil as their father. This may sound harsh or even cruel to the unsaved, but God's Word, the Bible, doesn't mince words. The child of God is in God's family, but the unbeliever is not. Even in the Old Testament, Nehemiah forbade the children of God from intermarrying with non-Jews.[7] As God's children, when we obey Him in this area, we will be inundated with His blessings in our relationships.

It is abundantly clear from Scripture, which is the depository of truth, that Christian marriages must be monogamous and between two believers only. Paul's instruction to the Corinthian and Roman brethren makes this point: "Stop forming inappropriate relationships with unbelievers. Can right and wrong be partners? Can light have anything in common with darkness...? Can a believer share life with an unbeliever?"[8] Another rendition of this verse is "Do not unite yourself with an unbeliever; they are not fit mates for you." To the Romans, Paul said, "I want us to help each other with the faith we have. Your faith will help me, and my faith will help you."[9] Having the same values and beliefs will foster mutual consent on questions ranging from "Where should we live to raise our family" to "Where should we worship God". Submitting to the authority of the Scriptures will serve as a guide to living a happy, fruitful, and productive life in the relationship. Finally, Amos makes the most potent argument, "Can two walk together except they agree?"[10]

As a marriage counselor, I've felt the pain of others as I listened to their horror stories. Many believers are mistreated and abused by their unbelieving spouses at home. Some of the stories are a graphic picture of hell on Earth. When it comes to marriage, please seek only for another believer. "She's at liberty to be married to whom she wishes, only in the Lord", and the same applies to the man.[11]

The Couple's Compatibility

When a couple engages in pursuing the same life goals, they become more unified, more focused, and are guaranteed to be a productive and winning team. The acrostic T.E.A.M. stands for Together Each Accomplishes Much. In this way, couples are focused on the same goals, moving in the same direction. Paul said, "For we are God's workmanship, created in Christ Jesus to do good works which God prepares in advance for us to do"[12], and "Each of you has a gift from God for serving others. Now you must be faithful to develop and use that gracious gift from God!".[13] When both partners use their God-given gifts to serve each other and those outside of their family, it fosters bonding within the home. Beyond the gifts, God wants us to know that our service is a holy calling. "Brothers and sisters, you are holy partners in a heavenly calling."[14] Let's remember that when God's instructions are obeyed and implemented, He receives the glory, and we receive the blessings, because His glory and our good are inextricably bound together.

Character Traits

Another key area which needs careful attention before marriage is the habits and conduct of your perspective partner. Watch out for these red flags:

1. Uncontrollable Anger: Scripture admonishes us, "Do not make friends with a hot-tempered man! Do not associate with one who is easily angered."[15]

2. Addicts: Again, we are warned, "Don't associate with people who drink too much or stuff themselves with food."[16] I must add, avoid people who are substance abusers, such as cocaine, marijuana, LSD, and other substances. Do not continue in that relationship unless there is a willingness to receive treatment.

3. Grudge Keepers: The Bible also warns, "Make sure you all have experienced the grace of God so that bitterness doesn't take root and grow, because that causes much trouble and will corrupt you."[17] It is significant to note that one of the most dangerous tools the Devil uses to break up marriages is the spirit of unforgiveness.

4. Selfishness: The root of all marital problems stems from selfishness. The Bible is unequivocal, "Selfish people cause trouble."[18] They cannot get along with anybody because the relationship is all about *them*. "People who do not get along with others are only interested in themselves; they will disagree with what everyone knows is right."[19]

5. Greedy People: One of the tentacles of selfishness is greed. In the Bible, we learn that a greedy man brings trouble to his family, so why partner with someone who's going to bring you trouble? We are admonished by the Scriptures, "Don't eat at the table of a stingy person."[20] Instead, practice the virtues of generosity and kindness because "A generous man will prosper; he who refreshes others will himself be refreshed."[21] "A kindhearted woman gains respect... and a kind man benefits himself, but cruel people bring trouble on themselves."[22] As a rule of thumb, every time we sow kindness, generosity, and goodness, we reap the same.

6. Laziness: A lazy person is unproductive and feeds on the backs of others. These are *freeloaders*. Paul, led by the Spirit, commands: "If anyone will not work, neither should they eat."[23] "Work hard and become a leader, be lazy and become a slave."[24]

7. Lack of integrity: Integrity is all encompassing. "I will be careful to live an innocent life. When will you come to me? I will live an innocent life in my house."[25] A person of integrity is also a truth-teller. As followers of Jesus Christ, we are called to walk in integrity and to maintain a clear conscience. When we keep our promises and honor our commitments, God and others will know that we walk in fellowship with Him. A person of integrity has everybody's trust, but one without

integrity stretches the truth, speaks half-truths, and lies. "A righteous person lives on the basis of his integrity. His children will be blessed even after he is gone."[26] What a legacy!

Before I got married to my best friend Grace, I humbly asked God for four specific things. First, my future wife needed to love Jesus more than life itself. She exceeds my expectations. Second, one of my dreams was to have a partner in ministry. She not only answered the call of God in her life, but continues to serve faithfully alongside me today. Third, another quality I desired was that of an exceptional nurse in our home to help me take proper care of our children. This desire came from an earlier hospital memory where my younger sister lost her first son due to the negligence of the staff on duty. The child was transfused with the wrong blood type and unfortunately passed away. Needless to say, I felt worried about the type of medical service that could make or break a growing family. Thankfully, my wife covers all the bases. Fourth, though not a necessity to me, it was a bonus that Grace and I are from similar ethnic backgrounds. Today, she is as stunningly beautiful as the moment I first met her.

Physical Attractiveness

While it is only natural to want someone who is physically attractive to you, you should also bear in mind that physical appearance should be the last criteria in choosing a mate. This suggestion to some may appear counter-cultural. Why? Unfortunately, our culture puts greater premium on physical attraction. It must be stressed that while good looks should be considered in your perspective mate, one must understand that our physical attraction fades away with time. Of course, beauty is in the eye of the beholder.

As a marriage counselor for over 25 years, I urge you to seriously consider the above character traits before proceeding in your relationship. If you sense that your partner is plagued with one or more of these emotional maladies, ending a dead-end dating relationship like this will be to your advantage. It can save you months, maybe even years of headache. "In the end, people appreciate frankness more than flattery."[27] Do not be fooled by appearances or be flattered by someone with a slick tongue. Let your life be guided by the Scriptures and prayers in this and in other areas, as you live your life for Christ. Furthermore, when choosing a life-partner, do not just consider their looks, talents, and financial assets. Ask the Lord for a discerning spirit to know if they have a controlling, vindictive, unforgiving, resentful, or slothful spirit. It is advisable that you seek help before making a commitment to enter the relationship.

Prayer: Lord, guide me in making this important decision about the person you want me to spend the rest of my life with. In Jesus' name, Amen.

Reflections on questions that will help you find the love of your life:

- Is your mate a believer?

- Are you compatible in these areas: spiritual, emotional, physical, and relational?
- Do they tend to abuse drugs, alcohol, or other harmful products?
- Do they have mood swings or a hot temper?
- How long have you been dating?
- Are you seeking marital counseling?
- What's unique about your partner?
- What kind of love do they exercise? Is it according to 1 Corinthians 13:4, 5, and 7?
- What reasons are motivating you to be married to this individual? (Some marry to get away from their parents, to make up a disappointment, or because of premature pregnancy)
- Do you think the marriage is God's will for your life?
- To those who've been divorced, what caused the divorce? What lessons did you learn from the first marriage? Will they help make you a better spouse?
- What evidence do you have to show that you've recovered from the hurts of your previous marriage?
- Do you have children from your previous marriage?
- Would your parents be an obstacle in your relationship?
- How well do you know your future in-laws? Do you get along with your future mate's parents?
- Are you considering living with/near either set of parents after you marry?

- Where will you spend your first Thanksgiving and Christmas after you marry?
- What have you done to let your parents know you love your mate?
- How often do you plan to visit or call your parents after you're married?
- Do you have any health issues? Do you plan to do blood tests before you get married? Have you had treatment for mental disorders or transmittal diseases?
- How much do you weigh? Is it an issue?
- Where do you plan to have your marriage ceremony and honeymoon?

CHAPTER 2

Oneness in God

"Therefore a man shall leave his father and mother and be joined to his wife, and they shall become one flesh."

(GENESIS 2:24)

In June 1994, the German brethren invited me to share the Gospel message in churches and youth rallies across Germany. After preaching for several weeks, my host wanted to give me a breather and drove us to a Mercedes-Benz plant where the cars are assembled. After an informative and memorable tour, we walked past the exit door to the parking lot when we witnessed a middle-aged man in rage, storming out of his car, arms flailing in anger. Shortly after he entered the plant, he was escorted out of the building by a service manager, leading him to his tailor-made car. Since the pair spoke in German, my host explained the situation to me. The middle-aged man did not know how to start his one-of-a-kind Mercedes. The service manager opened the car, took out the manual, and explained how to start the vehicle. As soon as he heard the roar of the engine, the ecstatic buyer drove off smiling from ear-to-ear.

This incident reminds me of how we should treat God's authoritative manual for marriage, the Bible. God, the designer, gives us a blueprint on how marriages work. Many ignore or are ignorant of God's instruction because they fail to consult His manual for marriage. Not only must a couple consult the Bible, they should intentionally apply its instructions to their relationship. The family should hold together like a braid of hair. It is impossible to create a braid with only two strands of hair (representing a man and woman). Two strands woven together will eventually unravel. Therefore, we need a third strand: God. The Bible tells us that the three-fold strand cannot easily be broken. Solomon says, "An enemy might defeat one person, but two people together can defend themselves; a rope that is woven of three strings is hard to break."[1] God is saying that two heads are better than one, but three are even better. In a marriage relationship, for two to grow in a lifelong union, God must be central to that relationship. He has all the resources, power, blessings, and desires to help the couple achieve the very purpose for which He intends — success in marriage.

Architect of Marriage

God created humanity for companionship with Himself and each other. He is also the source and divine architect of marriage. The family is His idea and He has a design in the Scriptures that makes it work. If understood and executed according to His plan, marriage will never end in divorce, experience dysfunctionality, or achieve mediocrity – it will thrive. Since no marriage is perfect, every union must encounter some tension or problems over time. Nonetheless, God has planned marriage to be the foundation of His Earthly kingdom.

A cursory observation of marriages around us shows that many relationships are failing. In a recent Billy Graham television classic broadcast, he said, "In America, one marriage out of three breaks down. In some parts of the country, it is one out of two. But where the family attends church regularly, the ratio is only one out of four. And if the family not only goes to church, but has a daily devotional life and family prayer regimen, the ratio of divorce is only one in forty marriages."

A recent national survey in Marriage Magazine reports that one out of every two and a half marriages ends up in divorce for both Christians and non-Christians alike. However, when a couple regularly attends church services together, reads the Bible together, and submits to the teachings of Christ, making Him the center of their relationship, only one out of 1,105 marriages ends up in divorce. In 1989, the New York Times reported a study showing that couples who have been happily married for long periods of time begin to look like each other. Even if the husband and wife bore no resemblance to each other on their wedding day, they show marked facial resemblance later in their marriage years. This resemblance is attributed to decades of shared emotional, physical, and spiritual habits.[2]

The divorce rate remains high because many marry for sociological reasons rather than theological ones. They marry for looks, money, and status instead of searching for God's match for their lives. Many people nowadays choose to ignore God's clear blueprint for marriage, preferring secular stereotypes presented by entertainers, the media, folklore traditionalists, sociologists, and pseudo-counseling experts. When conflicts arise, these counselors offer quick fixes for huge problems, like prescribing aspirin to cancer patients.

History of Marriage

God designed marriage to meet our need for person-to-person companionship. Per the Scriptures, history starts with marriage. The first human institution is based on God's first couple from the Garden of Eden: Adam and Eve. Civil government and the church also came from the mind of God, however, long before these were created, the family was first on God's mind. In the beginning, He looks at Adam and says, "It is not good for man to be alone." So He creates woman out of his rib, and our first family begins.

Since the family is God's idea, it operates best when man follows His design and follows His leadership. Marriage will not work if it is based on man's philosophy. Until all families make Christ the center of their homes, all human attempts to improve this union will end in frustration because, "Unless the Lord builds the home, we labor in vain in building it."[3]

The Bible not only talks about the first institution in the beginning, it ends with the marriage supper of the Lamb in Revelation – the great climax of all human history. The Bible teaches that human marriages end here on Earth, but in heaven we will be married to Christ for eternity. That's what all history is leading up to. When we cooperate with God, He will make us more like His Son Jesus. Then someday, at the best wedding ever, our Lord will present us to Himself as transformed beings – without spot or wrinkle – holy and without blemish.[4] This wedding will bring an end to all the sorrow, all the suffering, and the death that plagues our earthly, imperfect marriages. Since our Creator places a great premium on marriage, we should too. Therefore, it is crucial that we head into this divine union with great care and enthusiasm.

What is the Biblical Paradigm for Marriage?

Of the three models of marriage that exist today, only the third is the Biblical design:

1. Compact Marriage: A mutual agreement between two consenting adults – a man and woman – without parental or governmental approval.
2. Contract Marriage: A legally binding agreement between a man and a woman.
3. Covenant Marriage: A sacred or divine agreement between God and a couple.

God, by nature, is a covenant keeper.[5] In other words, God will never break His promises. The word "covenant" means an agreement or pledge between two or more parties. It contains terms that each party must perform to fulfill the agreement. However, covenants made with God are divinely binding, and once finalized, each party can be penalized for breaking their respective guidelines. It is significant to point out that the words "covenant" and "testament" are synonymous and are important to understand because the Bible comes to us in two testaments, the Old and the New.

Our focus in this chapter will be on God's covenant in marriage. God chooses to communicate to us, redeem us, and grant us eternal life in Jesus. The absence of Jesus makes both a covenant relationship with God and a covenant marriage impossible. So in this agreement, God demands real commitment on the couple's part – total, unreserved, whole-hearted devotion to each other. Since man, due to human limitations, has no choice but to rely on God's limitless ability to make the union work, we do not set the terms of the agreement, God does. Couples who ignore God's arrangement cannot find God's purpose for their marriage. Not only does a covenant agreement require total commitment, it demands sacrifice. Both the Old and New Testament covenants could not be made without a sacrifice – taking of life. In the Old Covenant, this meant sacrificing a lamb, goat, or sheep without a single spot or blemish. In the New Covenant, God gave His only Son as the sacrificial Lamb to be slaughtered.

The Lord's covenant with Abraham (known as Abram at the time), recorded in Genesis 15, depicts how animals were killed and "cut down in the middle and... [had their] halves [laid] side by side..." Only God "passed between the halves of the carcasses" because Abram saw all these things in a vision (v. 10); "So the Lord made a covenant with Abram that day." (v. 18) In God's Old Testament covenant dealings with mankind, He always kept His end of the bargain, but man would always break the covenant.

In the New Testament, however, God the Father made a covenant with His Son. Both the Father and Son are perfect, so they kept (and are keeping) the terms of their agreement perfectly. So basically, the New Testament is like the upgraded version of the old one. The author of Hebrews states, "Because of God's oath, it is Jesus who guarantees the effectiveness of this better covenant."[6] The New Testament is the final sacrifice that was created through the death of Jesus Christ on our behalf. The author of Hebrews further states, "For where there is a testament, there must also of necessity be the death of a testator. For a testament (covenant) is in force after men are dead, since it has no power at all while the testator (Jesus Christ) lives. Therefore, not even the first covenant was decided without blood."[7] Today, when we accept Jesus' death on our behalf by faith, His selfless sacrifice becomes our sacrifice. Paul declares, "One died for all, then all die; He died for all, that those who live should live no longer for themselves, but for Him who died for them and rose again."[8] That said, Christ's covenantal death is only valid if we accept His death as our own. "Now if we died with Christ, we believe that we shall also live with Him... For the death that He died, He died to sin once for all; but the life that He lives, He lives to God. Likewise, you also reclaim yourselves to be dead to sin but alive to God in Christ Jesus our Lord."[9] How does God do this? "God took the sinless Christ and poured into him our sins. Then, in exchange, He poured His power and goodness into us."[10]

Christian marriage is based on Christ's sacrifice made for us on the cross. Just as the Lord passed between the cut animals in Abram's vision, in marriage a man and a woman symbolically pass through the death of Jesus Christ which was done on their behalf into a totally new life and relationship with each other. This would have been impossible without His death. It is completely understandable to say that the covenant of the Christian marriage was made at the foot of the cross. Out of Jesus' death, new life is offered to all marriages.

Another great truth that is experienced in the covenant relationship is the aspect of intimacy. Through physical contact, we come together to bring forth new life that we share with each other. Without sex, there can be no fruit. Marriages that aren't consummated in sex are bound to remain sterile and lifeless. Thus, in a covenant union, the question to be asked is "What can I give?", not "What can I get?" This is the model of narcissism, which will be discussed later in this chapter. Without a covenant commitment and a sense of selflessness from both partners, God won't release his blessings and give His grace to us.

What is the Ultimate Purpose of Marriage?

Marriage from God's perspective is primarily designed to please and glorify Him and secondly, to make the two, one.

So, "In God's plan, men and women need each other."[11] The organizing principle for Biblical marriage is recorded in Ephesians. "Submit to one another out of reverence for Christ."[12] The key to a thriving covenant relationship is based on the connection that a husband and wife have for God first and with each other next. This approach can stand any challenge and overcome adversities that arise in the union. The solutions to overcoming every problem in marriage can be found in the true, relevant, and au courant (current) Scriptures in the Bible. When a couple understands the Bible's truths and applies its wisdom into their marriage, they will experience genuine oneness and 100% satisfaction. A second reason why marriage matters is for the multiplication of the human race. A further reason why marriage is important is for the protection of children. Kids grow up with a better chance of success in a two-parent home. These are better than an institution like an orphanage because the home is *supposed to be* a place of refuge and security. Another reason why marriage matters is for the perfecting of our characters. Our characters transform into the character of Christ over time in a solid marriage relationship. Marriage teaches us to love our spouse while dying to self. The home serves as a laboratory for character building. "So as iron sharpens iron, so a man sharpens the countenance of his friend."[13] Finally, the home also teaches us how to truly love. To cultivate a great marriage, our unions must reflect the marriage metaphor of Christ and His Church.

Three Great Truths

When Jesus comes to the region of Judea, the Pharisees approach Him, testing Him about divorce. Jesus replies, "From the beginning of creation, God made them male and female. Therefore, a man shall leave his father and mother and hold fast to his wife and the two shall become one flesh. So, they are no longer two but one flesh. What therefore God has joined together, let not man separate."[14]

Notice that God's overarching purpose is for the two to become one flesh. Jesus repeats it twice in these four short verses, and lays out three great truths for a lasting covenant relationship. First, Jesus said, from the beginning, God made them male and female. The chronology of events according to the Scriptures is that man is created first before woman. Both are made in His image to have fellowship with God. In Eden, God charges Adam with dominion over everything He created. There was an open corridor of communication from Eden to Heaven and vice versa. God told Adam to work in the garden. Man's assignment therefore was four fold: to have dominion, to cultivate, to keep, and to protect the garden. To relieve Adam of his loneliness, Eve was created from him, for him. Prior to Eve's grand entrance, Adam wasn't able to have a real relationship with any beast created in the garden. Eve was created for Adam to express love in the most intimate way. This includes procreating and filling the Earth with children made in God's image. In the final analysis, God intended the relationship between Adam and Eve to reflect the relationship between Christ and the Church.

Second, marriage is a union that involves two people, but Jesus said, "The two shall become one flesh." What does this statement mean? God's ultimate purpose for marriage is for two individuals with different personalities and backgrounds to become one (spiritually) with God and to become intimate, both physically and emotionally. However, a couple's goal of achieving unity and harmony with each other is hindered by our fallen human nature and lack of understanding of God's true purpose for marriage. The lack of commitment to God's marriage paradigm and an inbred narcissistic attitude stops us from forging a genuine spiritual relationship with God and our spouses.

Third, Jesus gives clear directives for His no-divorce-policy. "What therefore God has joined together let no man separate." Divorce is an affront to God's covenant plan in marriage, but today it occurs far too often. Here are the top ten reasons why people seek divorce:

1. *Incompatibility*: We aren't compatible intellectually, physically, and/or socially.

2. *Irreconcilable Differences*: We can't work things out – a contest of egos. Religious and cultural differences might destroy these relationships.

3. *No Communication*: We can't share our innermost feelings freely.

4. *Financial Problems*: We disagree too much about the way we spend our money.

5. *Hindrances in Occupational Growth*: We feel constrained because our marriage is holding us back from achieving our occupational goals in life.

6. *Distrust*: We don't trust each other like we used to. Jealously and insecurity are very present in our marriage.

7. *Unrealistic Expectations*: We want too much from each other.

8. *Unfulfilled Desires*: We fail to satisfy each other's emotional yearnings.

9. *Uncompromising*: We can't find middle ground in our challenging circumstances.

10. *Abuse*: We express abusive, controlling behavior in our relationship.

These problems can be mitigated or eliminated if we humble ourselves enough to understand and practice God's paradigm for marriage as presented in the Bible.

The Biblical Model for Oneness in Marriage

No close relationships are without conflict. We are dealing with two flawed, self-centered, imperfect human beings striving for intimacy. In other words, when two selfish people come together there are bound to be disagreements and clashes that can result in separation. However, God's oneness model only works when we live out our relationships in His way, using His plan. It should be noted that the true test of an intimate, strong relationship is not whether there is conflict, but how conflicts are resolved. We will discuss the details of this concept in the "win-Win-win Paradigm" in chapter 7. In the grand scheme of things, God's overarching goal is to bring sincere unity, happiness, and harmony in a covenantal relationship between a man and a woman. Fig. 1 below depicts the glue that will hold marriages together and overcome the barriers listed above.

Fig. 1

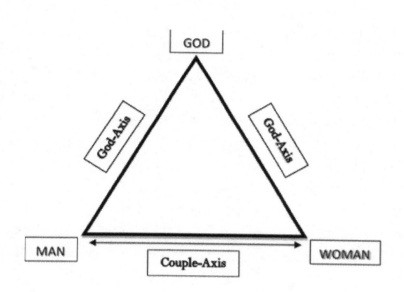

First, let's consider the Biblical formula for marriage between a man and a woman. God must be at the center of every relationship. That's the only way true unity can be experienced. Every couple should go by the formula: 1(man) + 1(God) + 1(woman) = 1(oneness). God created the man first. Then from the man's rib, He created the woman, and now He wants to unite them in a covenant marriage relationship to become one spiritually and emotionally, in thought and intent. In this model, the spouses submit to each other and are committed to each other. Marriage is a mysterious sharing and uniting of husband and wife with each other. The glory is in the mystery and joy of the two becoming one. When God is at the center of your marriage, you will live in harmony and love, and experience peace and true satisfaction. Our Biblical formula is fleshed out in the geometric model (Fig. 1).

Unlike humans, who don't have the required resources to carry out a divine task, when God tells us to do something, He also provides us with the resources to accomplish the task. When Paul wrote to the Philippians he said, "I can do all things through Christ who strengthens me."[15] A couple's dependence on God is a gift through which He draws them into an ever-deepening relationship with Him and with each other. The couple is trained to walk with the Holy Spirit, depending on Him every step of the way.

According to this model, there are two major routes the Christian couple must take to achieve oneness in the covenant relationship triangle. First, the man and woman must make progressive strides along the God-Axis. The pursuit of God is achieved through reading, meditating, and praying over God's Word together. During this time, they reflect and discuss what they have read and then look for ways to live out what they've learned. Then they bring the challenges they face in the relationship to the Lord in prayer and seek answers from God. During their Bible study time, each spouse can draw from the passage(s) to give them a broader, deeper understanding of God's character, plan, and promises for their home. In the time they spend in the Word of God, it's important to ask these questions: "What does this study reveal about our relationship?", "How can we treat each other in a way that glorifies God and deepens our love for each other?", and "Is there a promise to claim? Is there a command to obey? What example can I follow?" Encountering God in prayer requires both a listening ear and a receptive heart. In other words, when a couple spends time in the Word and in prayer, they discover who God is, what He says, and what truly pleases Him. Once they decide to give Him first place in their hearts and homes, their relationship will begin to blossom. Jesus said, "Seek ye first the kingdom of God and His righteousness, and all these things shall be added to you."[16] As a result, if the couple seeks God first in all things, by striving to delve deeper into His Word, then their actions and desires will be pleasing to Him.

Let's now consider the Couple-Axis in our Biblical model. Perhaps the greatest hindrance on the road to becoming one is narcissism (selfishness). Naturally, humans have excessive or egotistic interests in themselves and their own wellbeing. From birth we all inherited the same sinful nature. David said, "Behold, I was brought forth in iniquity, and in sin my mother conceived me."[17] Job had earlier declared, "Who can bring a clean thing out of an unclean thing? No one!"[18] Therefore, we can't naturally look out for one another without self-interest being involved. The root cause of self-interest is based on self-centeredness. Apostle James states, "What causes fights and quarrels among you? Don't they come from your desires that battle within you?"[19] This tendency shows itself in various ways: self-love, self-centeredness, self-focus, self-righteousness, selfishness, self-absorption, self-admiration, self-gratification, and egotistic behavior. Since trusting in ourselves is normal and rational to us, it makes it nearly impossible to cultivate an intimate, loving relationship with our spouse. Narcissism causes us to have an inflated view of ourselves, a deep need for self-admiration, and a lack of empathy for one another. True human nature says, "Life revolves around me, what I want is what I deserve." However, when we focus on others, we manifest selflessness, love, compassion, empathy, authenticity and humor in our covenant relationship. In other words, if selfishness destroys relationships, the antidote needed for intimacy is selflessness.

Paul encouraged the brethren of Philippi to capture and practice Jesus' spirit of humility through the help of the Holy Spirit. God's prescription for narcissism is, "Do nothing for rivalry or conceit, but in humility count others more significant than yourself. Let each of you look not only to his own interest, but also to the interest of others."[20] We can overcome our self-centered habits by dealing with our pride and humbly accepting what we don't deserve – the loving sacrifice of the Lord Jesus Christ on the cross. Thank God for your salvation, something we could never achieve by ourselves. In sum, as we submit and surrender to the indwelling Holy Spirit's control in every area of our lives, we please God and draw closer to each other in ways we could never have imagined.

With the Spirit's help, we can put to good use three practical ways of emulating God:

1. Giving

Jesus is the greatest sacrifice given to and for us, and no one can out-give Him. That said, giving makes us more like God. Since God is a liberal giver, He gives everybody what they need generously and ungrudgingly. He gave his very best when He sent his Son down to Earth to die for our sins. Paul calls God's present to us the "indescribable gift". The very breath, life, surroundings, and most importantly the eternal life through Jesus Christ are gifts from God that none of us deserve. By God's rules, every couple that decides to give of themselves first and share the things they possess with each other will experience happiness and harmony in their homes.

2. Forgiving

A second habit to cultivate is forgiveness. God forgave us of the sin debt that we couldn't pay by ourselves. He enables us to forgive our significant others whenever we feel like we have been wronged. As humans, we all offend each other by what we do and what we say, so repentance and forgiveness are essential to supergluing our broken relationships. Paul admonishes us to "Be kind to one another, forgiving one another, even as God in Christ forgave you."[21]

3. Serving

Jesus, our perfect example, came to seek and save the lost. Need an example? God came down in the person of Jesus and washed the disciples' feet with His own two hands. Being like

Christ calls for a lifetime of service in His name. Jesus said, "If I then, your Lord and teacher, have washed your feet, you also ought to wash one another's feet. For I have given you an example, that you should do as I have done to you."[22] When we engage to serve each other as man and wife, we put our spouse's interests above our own. Acting in each other's best interests kills selfishness in our own lives.

Some Practical Tips for Intimacy in Marriage

- Love your partner – drown your partner in affection because God did the same for us "while we were still sinners."[23]
- Treat your mate kindly – Start each day in friendly competition by intentionally trying to outperform each other in service to others and in good works.
- Always remember to forgive your mate compassionately.
- Seek your spouse's input on how you can make them genuinely happy each day. Let your spouse know that they are valued.
- Always offer compliments when deserved, but avoid criticism (nagging).
- Choose to focus on your partner's virtues and show appreciation for every kind act.
- Strive to agree by always finding a middle ground, and argue less.
- Endeavor to listen more and talk less.
- Endeavor to confess more and accuse less.

- Strive to laugh more and fret less.
- Give more of yourself and demand less of others.
- Overlook faults and let go of grudges.
- Although Jesus Christ is fully God, He chose to depend on the Father and the Holy Spirit working through Him to show us an example. We should do no less if we desire our marriages on Earth to reflect that of Christ and the Church.

This chapter's focus has been to present and discuss the Biblical paradigm for building oneness in a covenant marriage relationship. First, we try to understand the "great mystery"[24] about marriage. This mystery can only be learned by choosing to go through the process of spiritual initiation. You must follow God's blueprint for marriage as revealed in the Scriptures. Second, a self-serving outlook on life can be overcome through a covenant relationship when we practice putting the needs and interests of others at the forefront of our lives. A covenant marriage, therefore, requires total commitment, humble dependence on God, and death to our flesh daily. As a couple submits to the Spirit's control, they get to a point in the relationship where others can see God's image clearly reflected through them. Although marriage is difficult, any couple can live in love, peace, and harmony if God is at the center of it.

Prayer

Father, we confess that we are selfish by nature. Help us overcome our self-centered attitudes by dying to ourselves daily. May you be at the forefront of our lives through our thoughts, actions, and speech every day. May we also align our wills to Yours so that you may continue to increase while we continue to decrease.

Reflections on Oneness in Marriage

Fill in the blank spaces below:

She pulled her knees to her chest, feeling small and _____ once more.

1. Transparent
2. Restoration
3. Accountable
4. Vulnerable

He stood on the balcony, visible beyond the _____ curtains in the moving haze.

You will be held _____ if anything bad happens in this relationship.

It is certain that he took an active part in the _____ of their marriage.

For self-evaluation, list your current strengths and weaknesses:

Man (husband)
Strengths:

Weaknesses:

Woman (wife)
Strengths:

Weaknesses:

CHAPTER 3

Oneness in Vision: Seeing Each Other from God's Perspective

"Man knows himself only when he learns to understand himself in light of God, and he knows others only when he sees the mystery of God in them."[1]

– POPE BENEDICT XVI

"Every good gift and every perfect gift is from above, and comes down from the Father of lights, with whom there is no variation or shadow of turning."

– (JAMES 1:17)

Seeing with the Eyes of Faith

Whenever your spouse sees obstacles:
God Sees Opportunity

Whenever your partner sees faults:
God sees Growth

Whenever your mate sees problems:
God sees Solutions

Whenever your spouse sees closed doors:
God sees Open Doors

Whenever your partner sees life:
God sees Eternity

God's love for every couple is greater than any challenge they will face.

Throughout this book, each chapter will address an aspect of how we achieve the loving, lasting relationship that many seek today. Author and Pastor Charles Swindoll succinctly captures the essence of oneness when he writes, "If both husband and wife can apply grace to their marriage, their home will be a place of security and acceptance, of freedom and fulfillment, of accountability and encouragement." Before the Church, the state, the Laws of Moses, Abraham, and even before the Bible, marriage was an integral part of God's order.

When we look at things through God's perspective, we see less of our partner's weaknesses and more of their strengths. The hymn writer captures the essence of seeing each other from God's prism. David Allen writes:

Be Thou my Vision, O Lord of my heart
Naught be all else to me, save that Thou art
Thou my best Thought, by day or by night
Waking or sleeping, Thy presence my light
Be Thou my Wisdom, and Thou my true Word
I ever with Thee and Thou with me, Lord
Thou my great Father, I Thy true son
Thou in me dwelling, and I with Thee one
Riches I heed not, nor man's empty praise
Thou mine Inheritance, now and always
Thou and Thou only, first in my heart
High King of Heaven, my Treasure Thou art
High King of Heaven, my victory won
May I reach Heaven's joys, O bright Heav'n's Sun?
Heart of my own heart, whate'er befall
Still be my Vision, O Ruler of all.

Looking at each other from God's eyes as His gift makes all the difference in a marriage relationship. Seeing each other from God's lens is far superior than seeing each other from a human perspective.

Benefits Derived from a Marriage Relationship Come with Responsibility

To ensure a healthy, happy, and lasting relationship, God set in motion divine roles and responsibilities for the husband and wife. When a couple sees themselves in a covenantal relationship solely from a physical perspective, it is limiting. No matter how sexy you are, as the years go by, looks will ebb and fade. In contrast, a thriving relationship goes beyond physical appearances and takes root in the more important aspects of marriage: a well-nurtured spiritual and emotional connection.

Fig. 2

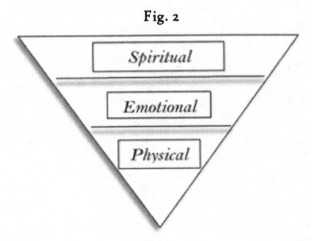

Figure 2 depicts the three most important components of a marital relationship. Generally, when people are looking for partners, they put the physical and emotional components of the relationship above the spiritual. The reason the triangle is upside down is because in a covenantal relationship, the spiritual component is more important than the emotional and physical appearance. Before we discuss the roles given to a man and woman, the couple must see themselves as gifts to each other from God. Solomon writes, "He who finds a wife finds a good thing and obtains favor from the Lord."[2] This is also true for a woman. James said it best, "Every good and perfect gift is from above, and comes down from the Father of lights..."[3] The next best thing that our Heavenly Father can give to a man or woman after salvation is a life partner. When a couple learns to hold each other at an immeasurable value, they will treat each other with the utmost respect and care. Think of a time in your life when you were given an expensive material gift. How much more care and respect should you treat your priceless, invaluable mate with? When the couple receives a genuine revelation of how priceless their mate is, the home will reflect God's desired plan. Jesus said, "Wherever your treasure is, there your heart [and thoughts] will also be."[4] On the contrary, if the couple does not value each other as priceless gifts from God, the home is doomed to failure. So ask yourself these questions: Do you think of yourself as valuable? Do you like yourself? Do you accept yourself? Do you forgive yourself when you blow it? Do you speak to yourself kindly (self talk)? A positive response to these questions reveals that you cherish who you are. Let's not forget, no one can see themselves in a negative light and accept others as they are. A positive perception of yourself will enhance your ability to see your significant other as a treasure. Remember, God loves you, just as you are. If a man or woman doesn't see themselves from God's perspective, they may not be able to fully love each other. God says, "You are fearfully and wonderfully made."[5] "You were knit together wonderfully in your mother's womb"[6], and, "you are God's treasured possession."[7] It's worth reiterating, you are valued by God, and His opinion of you is always accurate and always revealing the true beauty inside you. The Bible says, "The Lord does not look at the things man looks at. Man looks at the outward appearance, but the Lord looks at the heart."[8] Couples, see yourselves from Christ's perspective!

Author and pastor, Rick Warren, paints a vivid portrait of how God views you in his book The Purpose Driven Life: "You are not an accident. Your birth was no mistake or mishap, and your life is no fluke of nature.... Long before you were conceived by your parents, you were conceived in the mind of God. He thought of you first.... He custom-made your body just the way he wanted it. He also determined the natural talents you would possess and the uniqueness of your personality.... Most amazing, God decided how you would be born. Regardless of the circumstances of your birth or who your parents are, God had a plan in creating you. It doesn't matter whether your parents were good, bad, or indifferent. God knew that those two individuals possessed exactly the right genetic makeup to create the custom "you" he had in mind. They had the DNA God wanted to make you.... God never does anything accidentally and He was thinking of you even before He made the world.... This is how much God loves you and values you."[9]

To top it all off, God decided to deposit His love in your heart the moment you put your faith in Jesus Christ at conversion. His love guarantees that you can tap from an inexhaustible source of love to lavish on your mate. Paul observes, "Now hope does not disappoint because the love of God has been poured out in our hearts by the Holy Spirit who was given to us."[10] To every couple, Paul's prayer is "that the eyes of your heart may be enlightened"[11], to view each other as God's object of love.

Problems in Relationships

In today's marital arrangements, the traditional roles for the husband and wife are blurred. For some, men are afraid to be men, and women are ashamed to be women. Down through the centuries, women have been the pleasers, men the controllers. In many cultures, women are still the givers, while men continue to be takers. Most women show sympathy, compassion, and support, showing extraordinary availability when needed, while some men aren't in touch with their wife's feelings. Some men often take advantage, and the root of this is embedded in selfishness and greed. Sin, of course, has twisted the potentially beautiful interaction God intended into something grotesque, something that the Lord never intended. The Lord never expects women to please their husbands at ANY cost, neither does he intend for men to take advantage of their wives. The key to reversing this situation is to obey God's blueprint for the respective responsibilities that He's laid down for the husband and wife that must be infused and animated by grace.

The Roles of a Husband and Wife in a Covenant Relationship

When Adam was placed in Eden in Genesis 2:15, the first thing God gave man was His presence (Eden in Hebrew: "Where God dwells").

1. Presence — God wanted to have continuous fellowship with man, and for that to happen man had to be in His presence.

2. Work — God gave Adam a job with the job description. Adam was poised to cultivate and guard Eden.

> a) Cultivate – Man had to maximize and bring the best out of everything around him *including Eve*. That's why God never gave woman to man as a finished product. God's goal for every man is for his woman to flourish. So if your wife dresses shabbily, take her shopping. If she's getting a little "weighed-down" in life, encourage her to exercise more.

> b) Guard – To protect the plants, animals, and his wife, God gave Adam a strong bone frame and big muscles. He wasn't given that strength to punish his wife, but to love on her and cherish her with protection.

3. Word — God tells man not to touch of the tree of the knowledge of good and evil. It's important to point out that when God gives this command (Word) to man, Eve isn't in the picture. It then becomes Adam's responsibility to inform

Eve not to eat of the tree. When Satan came into the garden to tempt Eve, Adam was present and should've warned Eve to reject the Devil's temptation. When God came to visit them, He didn't ask Eve where they were. He called out to Adam, the man in charge. Whenever a woman asks questions, she's looking for knowledge and direction. The purpose of Eve being given to Adam was so that Adam would not be alone, for it is not good for man to be alone. In summary, man is to be constantly in God's presence. He is given a job and job description to cultivate, protect, and teach his woman His Word. Caution to women: if you meet a man who does not like to have constant fellowship with God or be in His presence, if he's not working, if he can't cultivate you, can't protect you, and can't teach you God's Word, leave that man alone. He's a man without a vision.

Writing to the Ephesians, Paul admonishes couples to "submit to one another in the fear of God."[12] To submit means to place one's self under the authority or command of another voluntarily. The couple will build a loving, God-centered home, if they both submit to God's authority. That's where it begins.

Husbands

To the man, Christ is saying, "Husbands, you want to be King in your castle? Follow my example." "Therefore, be imitators of God as dear children."[13] Essentially, God has four other basic responsibilities to the man towards his wife:

- *Husband as Head* – Paul instructs, "But I want you to know that the head of every man is Christ, the head of every woman is man, and the head of Christ is God."[14] Notice that Paul says the man (husband) is the head of the woman (wife). What does headship mean? It means that the husband has the ultimate responsibility for decision making and steering the direction the home ought to take. Considering the analogy of the physical body, decisions and direction on how the body functions come from the head (brain). Through the nervous system and in other ways, all parts of the body communicate with the head. The problem with many husbands today is that they make decisions and direct the activities of the home from their own ingenuity rather than depending on Christ, who IS their head. The man is also the spiritual head of the home, so he must be the one to lead his family in devotions and prayer.

- *Husband as Lover* – With Christ's indwelling love in the husband, he is able to love his wife unconditionally. "Husbands, love your wives, just as Christ also loved the church and gave Himself for her."[15] He sees her through the eyes of Christ, acts in her best interest no matter what, and his love covers her shortcomings. Not only does he love her unconditionally, but he loves her sacrificially. Christ gives Himself up for the church, "that He might present her to Himself a glorious church, not having spot or wrinkle or any such thing, but that she should be holy and without blemish" (v.27). If need be, the husband is willing to die for her and loves her carefully to such an extent that she wonders if she deserves such love. Finally, he loves her supremely, above all others except God. "So husbands ought to love their wives as their own bodies; because he who loves his wife loves himself" (v.28). This brief story exemplifies love: Bethany and Don Lansaw had just enough time to hide in their bathtub when a tornado struck down their home in Joplin, Missouri. As the vicious storm destroyed their entire neighborhood, the young husband shielded his wife with his own body. It was only after the tornado passed that Bethany realized Don had made the ultimate sacrifice. He had given his life to save hers.[16]

- *Husband as Provider* – In his first epistle to Timothy, Paul admonishes his protégé, "If anyone does not provide for his own and especially for those of his household, he has denied the faith and is worse than an unbeliever."[17] From the beginning, God made man to work in the garden to tend and protect it. So, the husband had a divine assignment from the beginning to be the nourisher: the financial and material provider to his wife and children. If he does not provide for his household, Paul uses very strong language, "He has denied the faith, and is worse than an unbeliever," – what an indictment!

- *Husband as Protector* – In his letter to the church in the diaspora, Peter says, "Show her honor as a fellow heir of the grace of life."[18] This verse points to equality and mutuality in the relationship – mutual and equal dignity, humility, and grace. When we offer this grace to one another, we are poised to make our homes a taste of Heaven. The rewards from deliberately putting these efforts into practice far outweigh the challenges that come with these efforts. Peter also commands, "Husbands, likewise, dwell with them with understanding, giving honor to the wife as to the weaker vessel, and as being heirs together of the grace of life that your prayers may not be hindered."[19] There are three aspects in this verse that we need to consider. First, the husband is instructed to live with his wife understandingly. He needs to put her interests above his own. Second, he is to honor her and not dominate her because she is physically weaker. Third, as a joint heir of the grace of life, he must work together harmoniously with her so that the full provision of God is made possible in their home. When a wife is abused and mistreated, or angry and frustrated with her husband, his prayers cannot be answered. However, when a woman feels secure, loved, cherished, and fully accepted by her husband, the home enjoys peace, harmony, and oneness. Therefore, husbands have the divine mission to be servant leaders, genuine lovers, faithful providers, and dogged protectors.

Wives

The wife's primary responsibility is to know herself so well and respect herself so much that her dignity and self-worth is rooted in her relationship with the Lord first, and then she can allow her husband to provide that support as the Lord develops him. She is also spirit-filled, thus willing to release her desires to control, to manipulate, to subvert, or to obtain what she desires through her own devices. She must trust that the Lord will meet her needs, which gives her enough security to give herself completely to her husband without reservation or hesitation. Essentially, the wife has two specific roles to fulfill for her husband:

- *Wife as Helpmeet* – From the beginning, after God created Adam, He realized that Adam was alone. He quickly solved that problem by creating Eve. God said, "It is not good that man should be alone; I will make him a helper comparable to him."[20] So Eve was created to help Adam fulfill God's mission on Earth: spiritually, emotionally, and physically. Every man looks to his wife for encouragement. I have been the beneficiary of my wife's love in my 25+ years in ministry, being that she's been the best encourager – not only in the ministry, but in our personal relationship as well. God has blessed me with a wonderful partner who helps to keep me focused on my calling. I can say unequivocally, wives, as you submit to and uplift your husbands, you are going to reap fruitfulness, joy, and harmony in your home.

- *Wife as a Support to the Head* – The man, as the head, cannot function without the body. He can't make decisions and set forth directions in the home by himself. Considering the analogy of the body to the family, the head is totally dependent on the neck, which represents the wife, to support him. Thus, the wife upholds, sustains, and nourishes her head. The wife not only plays this crucial role, but also determines and guides which direction the head turns. This role is carried out effectively ONLY when the wife submits to her husband. Peter admonishes "wives, to be submissive to your own husband, that even if some (the man) do not obey the Word, they without a word may be won by the conduct of their wives."[21] Notice that it is the wife's magnanimous, gentle, and tranquil spirit that inspires the husband to be genuinely masculine.

Practical Grace in Marriage

Willard Harley, in his book "His Needs, Her Needs"[22], gathered data from 20 years of counseling experiences. He conducted a survey of more than 15,000 questionnaires and his data revealed a distinct pattern that led him to generate two lists about the dichotomy of desires between men and women.

On one list, he noted that there were five primary relationship needs of a woman, and on the other, five primary relationship needs of men. Here is a summary of Harley's findings:

For Women

The first need they have is affection. Women crave affection that manifests itself in a tender, non-sexual expression of love. Verbal expressions should be accompanied with actions that range from a tender touch, a warm hug, a thoughtful note, and holding hands, to buying a beautiful bouquet of flowers. A touch can be intimate, but it must communicate that the husband values the wife as a precious person to him and not just for sexual gratification. The second desire women have expressed is in communication. Conversation between spouses sets the tone on how a wife feels loved, cared for, appreciated, respected, and wanted. For example, the man can express himself by saying, "I'll take care of you and protect you", "You are important to me", "I am deeply concerned about the problem you face", and "I think you are wonderful". Conversation to a woman is sometimes equivalent to what physical intimacy is to a man. The absence of communication, or very little of it, is emotionally devastating to a woman. She feels cast aside and wonders if he still loves her. The third desire is honesty and openness. Candid communication that accurately reflects the husband's deep feelings and motives are highly appreciated by the woman and draw her closer to her man. In addition, honest communication predisposes a woman to contemplate the future more accurately and to plan accordingly. Furthermore, when a man is completely open to his wife, the woman feels secure in the relationship. Fourth, financial support is essential for a woman to feel secure in the relationship. If there is sufficient financial provision, not including her earnings, the woman feels cared for, and safe from sudden poverty. Finally, but equally important, is family commitment. Women want their husbands to take a leadership role in the family because they were created to follow their husbands. So, they want men to lead and set an agenda without ignoring their input in the moral and educational development of their kids.

For Men

The number one desire for men is physical intimacy, in which the wife is actively engaged and satisfied. Sometimes, it is the man's desire that the woman takes the initiative to show the man that she desires him. Second, most men find pleasure in outdoor activities like fishing, going to a ball game, hiking, and working in the yard. They desire a playmate who they can enjoy life with, not only indoors but outdoors as well, so the wife is encouraged to take active interest in the husband's activities. The third aspect is an attractive spouse. Men admire women who take good care of their bodies and dress to be pleasing to their husbands. Men are more visual, so they like women who dress to kill and make him feel loved. Fourth, domestic support is another critical area that husbands yearn for. They desire wives who help in maintaining a tranquil and orderly home, because for the man the home represents a place of warmth, comfort, and peace – a shelter from the chaos that he faces each day outside of the home. The last but not the least need is a woman's admiration for her husband. When a man is praised and appreciated for wise judgment, abilities, and character, along with verbal expressions of respect (both public and private), it builds his self-esteem. For example, when a woman says to her husband "I respect you", to a man, that translates to "I love you".

The apostle Paul powerfully summarizes how a couple should treat each other. "To sum up, all of you be harmonious, sympathetic, brotherly, kind hearted and humble in spirit."[23] These are the qualities that ought to categorize couples in their relationship.

Prayer

Lord, in our own ability we can't carry out these key responsibilities. We ask for the help of the Holy Spirit to perform our divinely assigned tasks with joy and enthusiasm. We count on You because You've assured us in Your Word that it is "God working in [us], giving [us] the desire to obey Him and the power to do what pleases Him."[24]

Reflections on Oneness in Vision

- As much as it depends on you, focus on your own God given responsibilities, not on your spouses.
- Don't try to change your spouse, because only God can do the job of transforming us by His Spirit. "God will make you complete in every good work to do His will, working in you [and through you],

what is well-pleasing in His sight, through Jesus Christ, to whom be glory for ever and ever. Amen."[25]

- Pray for each other daily and together as often as you determine, reflecting on each other as gifts from God.

- List some creative ways you can spend time together.

- In what ways can you be a positive support to your spouse as each person tries to carry out his or her God-given assignments?

CHAPTER 4

Oneness in Communication

"O my dove, in the clefts of the rock, in the secret places of the cliff, let me see your face, let me hear your voice; for your voice is sweet, and your face is lovely."

(SONG OF SOLOMON 2:14)

Healthy communication in marriage is the bridge between confusion and clarity. A marriage counselor once said that the lack of good communication accounts for 80% of all marital problems. It therefore becomes obvious that couples must work hard at the art of effective communication. Marriage does not create problems, nor is it a panacea for resolving relational problems. It only reveals our individual, ill-equipped skills in communication that we bring into the relationship. It also magnifies our concealed selfishness. So, it is safe to conclude that if we trace our marital problems back to their source, we'd discover that most of our problems are rooted in ineffective communication.

The Bible warns us that poor communication is more destructive to any relationship than any other problem in marriage. King Solomon speaks pointedly about the control that words have over our lives: "Death and life are in the power of the tongue, and those who love it will eat its fruit."[1] The apostle Peter echoes these sentiments when he says, "If you want a happy life and good days, keep your tongue from speaking evil and keep your lips from telling lies."[2] When good communication prevails in the home, it keeps the couple strong and healthy, and brings them closer in a common bond. However, where poor communication exists, a marriage is headed for the rocks.

Communication experts have identified five levels of communicating. The first level is the frivolous level. At this level, the conversation is centered on small talk. The primary topics of discussion reflect on everyday occurrences like weather, sports, and clothing, just to mention a few. The next level is the factual level. Discussions here focus on facts, such as news reports, current events, and hot topic issues. Third is the fellowship level. Discussions here delve into critiques, ideas, making judgments, and taking strong positions on vital issues. When debates get heated over ideas, judgments, and philosophies, there is a tendency for one party to retreat. Fourth is the feeling level. Not only do we talk about ideas, judgments, and philosophies, here we open up and say how we feel about sentiments expressed in the conversation. Depending on the topic of discussion, we tend to either hurt or affirm their positions. Last is the freedom level. Discussants at this level share their deep fears, dreams, and ideas openly without fear of rejection or retribution. It is the desire of communication experts that couples will eventually get to this last level because it promotes trust and creates a genuine bond between partners.

Bad Habits to Avoid in Communication

There are four distinct areas that must be avoided during communication in a marital relationship. These include:

1.   *The Silent Treatment* – When a spouse is hurt, they refuse to speak to their partner.
2.   *Divorce* – The threat of divorce should never be mentioned in a marital relationship. Once divorce is used as a threat, it builds distrust in the relationship, which may be hard to rebuild.
3.   *Sex* – Never use sex as a weapon to punish your partner.
4.   *Curses* – The use of curse words, insults, and foul language will eventually cause irreparable damage in a marital relationship. Hence, care must be taken to use appropriate words in our daily conversations.

Guidelines in Effective Communication

A model of intimate, loving communication for couples is recorded in Song of Solomon, where King Solomon and the

Shulamite, his bride, talk to one another in endearing terms. Words of intimacy that deal with the innermost part of their hearts are frequently used as they express their thoughts, dreams, fears, secrets, failures, and aspirations. This type of communication is exclusive to husbands and wives and cannot be shared with others. This indeed is the secret to lasting relationships. They praise and affirm each other in three areas: physical attraction, emotion, and intellect.

Plentiful Words

These two talk to each other... A LOT. Almost 65% of the verses in Song of Solomon are composed of intimate dialogue. They speak to each other candidly, openly, romantically, and without embarrassment. Husbands and wives today need to develop these good unrestrained habits. Many wives desire that their husbands talk to them at this level but sometimes receive the silent treatment.

Astronaut Michael Collins once observed that in an average day, a man speaks about 25,000 words while a woman hits 30,000. He surmises that before the man gets home after work, he has used up most of his words, so when he returns, he has fewer words to share with his wife. To stop the marriage from growing colder due to lack of communication, it is advisable that a man look for creative ways to speak more. In addition, a vast majority of women rank security as their #1 priority in the relationship. The only way to truly sustain the feeling of security for the female is to have constant, oscillating conversation between the partners. Since they crave meaningful, intimate dialogue, it would be vital for men to make conversation a priority in marriage.

Personal Words

The pet names that we create for our spouses can be great ways to deepen a bond and make each other feel special. Solomon and his bride had pet names for each other too. Solomon's bride calls him, "My dove, my perfect one."[3] He replies and calls her, "My beloved, white and ruddy, the chiefest among ten thousand"[4], as well as, "my love, lovely, and awesome,"[5]. Clearly, they value each other as #1 in their lives. Furthermore, not only are the words of Solomon and his Shulamite wife plentiful and personal, they are positive.

Positive Words

Notice how positively they speak to each other. No negative or critical words are expressed towards each other during their conversation. While negative words ruin relationships and create walls between couples, encouraging words bring them closer to each other. Paul, in his letter the Colossians, says, "Let your speech be always with grace, seasoned with salt."[6] As salt flavors the taste to food, so too does grace add flavor to our speech. Salt is also a preservative, so speech that comes out of the nature of grace will preserve the marriage. Another key element in the area of communication that fosters intimacy is showing acceptance and showering compliments on each other. The Shulamite woman demonstrates these concepts by saying, "His mouth is sweet; yes he is altogether lovely. This is my beloved, and this is my friend...."[7]

For over the twenty-five years I have spent as a marriage counselor, I have observed that the need for intimacy is crucial. During one of my many sessions, a lady said, "The only time my husband compliments me is when he wants food, sex, or the channel changed."

Eight Effective Ways to Communicate with your Spouse

The Scriptures provide certain guidelines to enhance communication in a marital relationship:

1. *Be Polite* – Be intentional with the words you speak to your lover, considering each other's feelings. "Don't use foul or abusive language. Let everything you say be good and helpful, so that your words will be an encouragement to those who hear them."[8] As much as it depends on you, avoid name-calling, threats, interruptions, and yelling at each other. These types of words are stepping stones to breaking up a good relationship.

2. *Be Affirming and Complimentary* – Always look for little things that your mate does to encourage them in the relationship. For example, "Thank you for ironing my clothes, sweetheart" or "I appreciate that you made the bed this morning." "From a wise mind comes wise speech; the words of the

wise are persuasive. Kind words are like honey, sweet to the soul and healthy for the body."[9]

3. *Be Sorry* – Because we can never attain perfection in this life, we will sometimes rub each other the wrong way. The solution is to quickly say, "I'm sorry" and to say it sincerely. Those three little words, said from the heart, can heal big emotional scars. "A gentle answer deflects anger, but harsh words make tempers flare."[10]

4. *Be Attentive* – Good communication involves developing listening skills and repetition to avoid misunderstanding. It is also advisable to maintain good eye contact during conversation. "Understand this, my dear brothers and sisters: You must all be quick to listen, slow to speak, and slow to get angry."[11] There was a time in my first year of marriage when my wife was telling me a funny story while we were watching TV. Unfortunately, my ears were only half listening to her, while my eyes were fixed on the NBA finals. Before I knew it, she got up from the chair and stood exactly between the TV and me. That day, I learned my lesson very quickly: even when excitement is at its peak and the world is going haywire, my wedding ring is still more important than the NBA Championship ring.

5. *Be Open* – Overtly share your deepest feelings to your partner without any reservations. As a reminder, communication with your spouse

deepens your relationship and draws you closer together. "Gentle words are a tree of life; a deceitful tongue crushes the spirit."[12]

6. *Be Truthful* – By far, the most important aspect in communication is being frank and candid because these virtues (above all others) build trust in the relationship. Remember, truthfulness always brings trust. "Gentle words are a tree of life; a deceitful tongue crushes the spirit."[13]

7. *Be Timely* – As much as it depends on you, when you make a commitment, make sure you accomplish your task within an acceptable time frame. Always find time to talk to each other without interruptions from people or things. "Everyone enjoys a fitting reply; it is wonderful to say the right thing at the right time!"[14]

8. *Be Creative* – Proactively and intentionally inject humor, and lots of it, in your conversation. Tell each other funny stories about what you've been through or what you've heard. Look for little things that will lighten the mood. Do not take things, or yourself, too seriously. Be curious about each other's day. Endeavor to focus less on budgets and deadlines but more on each other. Focus more on counting your blessings since you got married, and dreaming big about the future.

In sum, effective communication is the lubricant that enhances good dialogue in marriage. It's imperative to set boundaries beforehand by establishing areas that are off limits in the conversation, such as: avoiding the use of the D-word (divorce), using abusive language, using sex as a weapon, and refusing to talk to your spouse.

Prayer Tip

Memorize these verses:

"A gentle answer deflects anger, but harsh words make tempers flare."

(PROVERBS 15:1)

"Gentle words are a tree of life, a deceitful tongue crushes the spirit."

(PROVERBS 15:4)

Lord, help me to control my speech.

Reflections on your Marital Communication Skills

Fill in the blank: Never use _____ as a weapon to punish your partner.

Answer this question: Discuss 4 areas that must be avoided during communication (pg. 77)

CHAPTER 5

God's Financial Management Plan

"Whoever loves money never has enough; whoever loves wealth is never satisfied with their income. This too is meaningless."

(ECCLESIASTES 5:10)

God has a financial plan for His children. It's found in His Word. Money is one of life's major issues – an issue that deserves serious consideration and planning for any couple to live happily. There is an adage that states, "To fail to plan is to plan to fail." Many couples are proving the truth of this maxim because they fail to properly plan how they will manage their finances.

God Owns Everything

When examining God's plan, let's first establish that the source of all wealth is God, as declared by the Scriptures. God's message through Job states, "...Everything under Heaven is [God's]."[1] The psalmist also observes that "The Earth is the Lord's, and everything in it. The world and all its people belong to Him."[2] Haggai further states, "The silver is Mine, and the gold is Mine, says the Lord Almighty."[3] The above texts point us to the one and only source of money: the God who owns it all.

From the beginning when God created the Heavens and the Earth, He gave man dominion over all created things to manage them. Man became the caretaker, or steward, of God's Earth.

Man, God's Steward

As God's land agents, what must our attitude be towards the gold and silver entrusted to us? Paul warns us not to love money: For, "The love of money is at the root of all kinds of evil and some people, craving money, have wandered from the faith and pierce themselves with many sorrows."[4] Notice that Paul does not say that acquiring money is evil, rather, craving money leads to heartache and despair. Money is a tool that Christians need to use to acquire goods and services. Another warning that Paul gives is for Christians not to be miserly or stingy; we are supposed to reflect the nature of God by our generosity, giving proportionally and not out of compulsion. When, "God's people give generously to the poor, their good deeds will never be forgotten."[5] In addition, when we obey God in giving, He promises us an abundance of wealth in return. Luke writes, "Give, and you will receive. Your gift will return to you in full-pressed down, shaken together to make room for more, running over, and poured into your lap. The measure you give will be the measure you get back."[6] The lesson learned in these verses is to give proportionally without grudging, but with exuberance. Good financial planning will prevent economic crisis, prevent a believer's spiritual stagnation, and open doors for spiritual maturing.

Setting Priorities

When He preached at the Sermon on the Mount, Jesus established fundamental Christian principles when he stated, "Seek ye first the kingdom of God and His righteousness, and all these things shall be added to you."[7] This admonition applies to every facet of the Christ follower's life and is especially important in the financial affairs of a believer. Christ must take first place in our lives.

The essence of Christian financial planning priorities can be found in James' letter to the diaspora. "Look here, you who say, 'Today or tomorrow we are going to a certain town and will stay there a year. We will do business there and make a profit.' How do you know what your life will be like tomorrow? Your life is like the morning fog – it's here a little while, then it's gone. What you ought to say is, 'If the Lord wants us to, we will live and do this or that.' Otherwise you are boasting about your own pretentious plans, and all such boasting is evil."[8]

Since money is a gift from God, even though we earn it through hard work, it is imperative that we seek God's will (through prayer) for the money we make to avoid heartache, pain, and financial disappointment. After all, the idea of and energy to make wealth comes from God. "Remember the Lord your God. He is the one who gives you power to be successful..."[9] Not only does God give you the ability to create wealth, it is He who teaches you to profit.

Personal Commitment

To be a good steward as God expects, every believer must be committed to take a proactive stand to get out of financial dilemmas. Christian couples must genuinely desire to get their financial "house" in order. To achieve financial equilibrium and success, the couple must forgo some of their poor spending habits and be prepared to accept some pain in eliminating the non-essentials in their planning and purchasing of goods and services.

Agur prays, "First, help me never to tell a lie. Second, give me neither poverty nor riches! Give me just enough to satisfy my needs. For if I grow rich, I may deny you and say, 'Who is the Lord?' And if I am too poor, I may steal and thus insult God's holy name."[10]

From these verses, we can glean two powerful truths for financial success. The first ingredient in obtaining meaningful prosperity and success is obedience to God's Word. Mary, the mother of Jesus, tells the servants at the wedding feast of Canaan, "Whatever He says to you, do it."[11] Obeying God's order always brings a blessing. Second, being in God's will requires that we keep his decrees, commands, laws, and requirements for our lives. Like the prophet Samuel told King Saul, "To obey is better than sacrifice, and to heed better than the fat of rams."[12] As a Christian couple, avoid impropriety or short cuts to prosperity at all costs. Genuine success comes only by walking in His Ways and obeying His Word.

God's Financial Game Plan

To achieve success with God's financial plan, the couple must bring their needs before God, seeking His will. Many Christians skip this step and make their own decisions, then ask God to bless what they've planned instead of submitting to God's leadership first.

Financial planning, God's way, eases the frustration of economic instability that many couples experience. God's desire for each of His children is to dwell in the land of "more than enough". In this land, the couple not only has the capacity to take care of themselves, but to also serve as a conduit of blessings to others. However, as affluence grows, the Christian must watch out for signs of greed, covetousness, or hoarding wealth. These practices will not only create distrust within the marriage, they may also lead to financial disaster. The Bible warns, "Lay not up for yourselves treasures upon Earth... But lay up for yourselves treasures in heaven... for where your treasure is there your heart is also."[13] "Since everything around us is going to melt away, what holy, Godly lives should we be living?"[14] Therefore, watch out for half-hearted commitment. Full surrender to God's purposes and will is the key to financial prosperity.

There are several methods a Christian can use to manage God's money. We will be discussing two methods, God's Financial Blueprint (GFB) and Supernatural Debt Cancellation. Using a Microsoft Excel program, you can easily tabulate your income according to the GFB guidelines as indicated in the table below.

God's Financial Blueprint

Items	Percentage
Generous Offerings	11-15
Housing (Rent/Mortgage)	15-20
Food	15-20
Medical Care	5-10
Savings (Short/Mid/Long-term)	15-20
Recreation/Vacation	5-10
Debt Payment	2-5
Clothing	2-5
Personal Care/Miscellaneous	2-4
Total Income	100

The GFB shows a breakdown of the essential partitions necessary to manage God's money. It is highly advisable that a similar percentage be given both to Generous Offerings and to Savings. Since tithing is not a New Testament teaching, we use the term "Generous Giving", which is clearly taught in the N/T. Paul, writing to the Corinthians, instructs in the passages cited that the attitude of giving matters more than the amount given. Therefore, they were urged to give hilariously and generously. God will not accept gifts that are given grudgingly, neither will He bless those who sow sparingly. There are, however, great benefits to receive when we give from our hearts.

Jesus says, "If you give, you will receive. Your gift will return to you in full measure, pressed down, shaken together to make room for more, and running over. Whatever measure you use in giving – large or small – it will be used to measure what is given back to you."[15] Paul echoes Jesus' admonition when he says, "And this same God who takes care of me will supply your needs from His glorious riches, which have been given to us in Christ Jesus."[16] Having Christ's glorious riches will provide you with everything you need so that there will be nothing broken, missing, or lacking in your life – our God is the God of more than enough.

It is important that money be set aside, as illustrated in the GFB, for savings. We save for unexpected emergencies and expenses, and we invest for retirement purposes. The guidelines on our GFB, as reflected in the percent ranges, are intended to be flexible according to the individual's preferences. It is not enough to only talk about how money is spent in your home; there needs to be a financial plan so that the couple can provide an accurate account of how their money was spent. As good stewards of God's money, we will be held accountable on how we spent the money entrusted to us. With the help of a guide such as the GFB, many of the problems associated with financial mismanagement in the home can be greatly minimized.

Supernatural Debt Cancellation

What do you do as a believer when you are steeped in financial crisis? The first and foremost thing to do is to get a job to bring in income. If you are already working, place a temporary freeze on your spending habits. If the GFB model doesn't work, then employ the Supernatural Debt Cancellation paradigm (SDC). While the GFB operates on strict discipline, the SDC is faith based. The Scriptures presents us with an example of the faith based model in the narrative of Prophet Elisha and a widow in 2 Kings. This widow's husband dies and leaves her with a huge debt. She reports that creditors have threatened to take away her two sons as slaves as a payment for the debt her husband owes. She approaches Elisha and asks for help to which he replies, "What can I do to help you?" Before the lady responds, he asks a follow-up question. "Tell me what you have in the house." The widow replies, "Nothing at all except a flask of olive oil." Elisha instructs her to borrow as many empty pots as she could from her neighbors and friends. She was further commanded to go into her house "shut the door and fill the empty vessels with her jar of oil."[17] After that, she was commanded to sell the oil and pay off her debt and use the rest of the money to support her and her sons. We can glean four principles from this narrative.

1. Go to God in prayer with your heavy debt burden and pray the prayer of faith. The Bible says the "effectual fervent prayer of the righteous man avails much."[18]
2. The second step is to sow a seed of faith to a church or to a Christian organization.
3. Third, *believe* that God will take your limited resources and exponentially exceed your needs.
4. "The Lord promises believers that... by his mighty power at work within us, He is able to accomplish infinitely more that we would ever dare to ask or hope."[19]

Benefits of a Financial Game Plan

In sum, there are several benefits to derive as we follow up on the GFB and SDC models. First, it prevents suspicion between the couple in the home regarding their finances. Second, it deters the couple from getting into debt because it prompts them to live within their means. Finally, they will be able to monitor their spending habits since they have a guide to follow. God's promise is, "Don't be obsessed with getting more material things, I'll never let you down, never walk off and leave you."[20] With the GFB and SDC models, the couple can grow into being responsible and accountable stewards with the money that has been entrusted to them by God. By working on these models, even though financial crises, the couple can grow closer to God and to each other.

Prayer

- Whenever you receive your income, make sure you pray over the money.
- "Lord, help me to be a generous giver to Your work and to those in need."

Tip

- Without a GFB model, you are heading for financial disaster.
- Don't plan and then ask God to bless your plan. Always pray before planning.

Reflections on your Financial Management

- What are your current habits regarding credit cards, bank accounts, stocks, and investments?
- What factors do you consider when making large financial purchases?
- Do you have plans to invest in property, stocks, or bonds?

CHAPTER 6

Intimacy in Marriage

"Let marriage be held in honor among all, and let the marriage bed be undefiled, for God will judge the sexually immoral and adulterous."

(HEBREWS 13:4 ESV)

Adultery is the most evil act in marriage because many are obsessed with sex. We live in a sex-saturated culture where many people dress provocatively. Magazines, newspapers, online sites, and other media outlets are sources of sexual advertisement. The purpose of sex by its designer (God) is for enjoyment and intimacy. It creates a strong bond between a husband and wife. Sex is also given to us for pleasure and procreation, given that humans are the crown jewels of God's creation.[1] Sex involves every aspect of our being. It involves total oneness with our mates, just as it did with the first couple: physically, yes, but also psychologically, emotionally, and spiritually. That's why sex before marriage is unhealthy. God designed sex to bring people together in an intimate, exclusive union. God created sex as a sacred act between two committed people. Because of its sacredness, the expression of love and oneness between a husband and wife must be protected and honored. According to the writer of Hebrews, "Marriage is to be held in honor by all, and the marriage bed is to be undefiled."[2] The sexual union goes even deeper than honoring the marriage bed because intercourse between a man and a woman symbolizes the way God interacts with His people. As an act of incredible love, God seeks intimacy with us. Let's cite an example from Scripture of a man who fell because of sexual infidelity.

David the King, whom God called a man after His own heart, fell into sexual immorality. The prophet Samuel describes David's fall into sexual sin, "In the spring of the year, when kings normally go out to war, David sent Joab and the Israelite army to fight the Ammonites. They destroyed the Ammonite army and laid siege to the city of Rabbah.

However, David stayed behind in Jerusalem. Late one afternoon, after his midday rest, David got out of bed and was walking on the roof of the palace. As he looked out over the city, he noticed a woman of unusual beauty taking a bath. He sent someone to find out who she was, and he was told, 'She is Bathsheba, the daughter of Eliam and the wife of Uriah the Hittite.' Then David sent messengers to get her; and when she came to the palace, he slept with her. She had just completed the purification rites after having her menstrual period. Then she returned home. Later, when Bathsheba discovered that she was pregnant, she sent David a message, saying, 'I'm pregnant'." This passage shows us how sexual temptation works. Here we see a king who was supposed to be at war, yet he stayed behind and caught himself in the snare of temptation. He knew very well that this was the wife of Uriah the Hittite. He willfully ignored his good conscience and lusted after somebody else's wife. He lay with her, and as a result got her pregnant. When David got word that Bathsheba was with child, he devised a plan to cover it up: he asked that Uriah be recalled from the battlefield. When he saw Uriah, David asked him how the war was going and then commanded him to go back to his house to sleep with his wife. Uriah disobeyed the king's order. His conscience wouldn't let him enjoy himself while his friends were out in battle. To cope, Uriah slept in the quarters of all the other servants near the king's door. When David's plan didn't work, he made matters worse by coaxing Uriah to drink and attempting to persuade him that home was better than the castle, but Uriah refused. Finally, he wrote a letter to Joab (the captain) to send Uriah to the most dangerous forefront of the battle to be killed. Joab obeyed the king's instructions, and Uriah was killed.[3]

In contrast, Joseph defeated sexual temptation by fleeing from it. The narrative is found in Genesis, which says, "[Potiphar's wife] came and grabbed him by his cloak, demanding, 'Come on, sleep with me!' Joseph tore himself away, but he left his cloak in her hand as he ran from the house. When she saw that she was left with only his cloak, she called out to her servants. Soon all the men came running. 'Look' she said. 'My husband has brought this Hebrew slave here to make fools of us! He came into my room to rape me, but I screamed'."4 That lie got Joseph thrown quickly into jail. The twist is that although he went through great trials, this one being counted among the largest, Joseph stayed patient, trusted God, and ended up being positioned as the Prime Minister of Egypt. The lesson to be learned in overcoming sexual sin is to run away from it. Paul instructs, "flee sexual immorality. Every sin that a man does is outside the body, but he who commits sexual immorality sins against his own body."5 In the same literary breath, Paul bade Timothy to flee sexual temptation. "Flee also youthful lusts: but follow righteousness, faith, charity, peace, with them that call on the Lord out of a pure heart."6 The lesson to learn here is to get out of the path of sexual temptation.

Here are some practical steps that couples should integrate in their marriages to avoid embarrassing escapades.

- Do not have intimate conversations with anyone who's not your spouse.
- Avoid sending seductive texts to anyone who's not your spouse.
- Run away from sleazy men and women who try to seduce you.
- Don't give in to sexual innuendos.
- Don't watch pornographic images on your computer, phone, or game console.

The Consequences of Infidelity

Sexual immorality, in many instances, results in divorce, and a broken home, more often than not, produces dysfunctional children. When kids grow up in a home without their father, many become social liabilities. These statistics are telling[7]:

- 72% of the nation's teen murderers come from fatherless homes
- 70% of long term prison inmates grow up in homes without dads
- 60% of people who commit rape were raised in homes where fathers were absent

These shocking reports go a long way to prove that America must go back to God's original design for sex. God created this beautiful relationship for procreation, pleasure, and our protection. We need to flee temptation and sexual immorality, returning to purity in sex. We also need to proactively determine, with the Spirit's help, not to give in to sexual innuendos at our jobs, not to give in to sexual advances with our neighbors, and not to peer at inappropriate images from bright screens. As we mentioned earlier, sexual intimacy outside of a relationship can devastate trust between the husband and wife as well as their sex life. Let's be careful, your body will follow where your eyes are focused – flee sexual temptation.

In contrast, a major element in *building* an intimate sexual relationship is timing. Speaking to each other in amorous terms and using intimate code words set the stage for greater satisfaction and intimacy. One reason why so many marriages are failing is that spouses react to each other from their minds, rather than from their hearts. When your wife says "I feel depressed." Listen to her; It's legitimate. When your husband says, "I don't think this is the right thing for us to do." Listen to his guidance. Listening to each other's heart is crucial because love begins with an understanding heart. "God's love has been poured out into our hearts through the Holy Spirit who has been given to us."[8] Your responsibility is to yield, submit, and surrender to the indwelling presence of the Holy Spirit daily, so that He will live His life through you. Understanding why others feel the way they do goes a long way in enhancing a relationship. Ask questions and then listen. Hear the hurt and the pain. Seek to understand the problem, and know what makes them tick. You need to know the mood of the person closest to you.

To the Couple

Listen to Paul's admonition, "Nevertheless, because of sexual immorality, let each man have his own wife, and let each woman have her own husband. Let the husband render to his wife the affection due her, and likewise also the wife to her husband. The wife does not have authority over her own body, but the husband does. Likewise, the husband does not have authority over his own body, but the wife does. Do not deprive one another except with consent for a time that you may give yourselves to fasting and prayer, and come together again so that Satan does not tempt you because of your lack of self-control."[9] Each person should regard their bodies as belonging to their mate, and not under their own total control to use however they please. Solomon, in Song of Solomon, declared that romance needs attention. He said, "Even much water cannot put out the flame of love."[10] Here, he advises that the couple pay attention and proactively develop healthy boundaries within the relationship: this is how our physical and emotional needs are met. Don't go to bed angry; always make amends before the sun goes down. Pray together every day. Pray before you have intimacy, because intimacy with the Lord inspires intimacy with each other. Have a joint Facebook page with your wife. Again, avoid watching pornography on your computer, phone, or game console.

To the Husband

Husbands must listen to these seven romantic needs for his wife. As we all know, romance is spelled R-E-L-A-T-I-O-N-S-H-I-P. First, the woman needs to receive spiritual nourishment from her husband. She needs protection as well as spiritual leadership in the home for the wellbeing of her soul. Second, she needs a safe and secure environment. Third, she needs constant assurance of the husband's love. She needs assurance that they will stay married and in love, unconditionally. The Shulamite woman (the object of Solomon's passion) said, "I am my beloved, and my beloved is mine."[11] Clearly, we see here that Solomon's wife had a strong sense of contentment and security. Fourth, the woman needs the sharing of intimate conversation with her husband. She desires to be his best friend and to have deep intimate conversations about the way they both feel. One-word answers will not cut it. When a woman asks her husband "How was your day", "Fine" is never the only response; women need a constant touch with gentle words to feel loved. For instance, an arm placed around her shoulder, with a hug and a kiss, speaks the language of love from the wife's perspective. Gentle caresses of the face, followed by words like "I love you sweetheart", and lavishing her with praise and compliments contribute to the wholeness and wellbeing of the relationship. Fifth, women need to feel pursued and set apart by the man. Do things that will sweep her off her feet. You can buy her flowers one day, pen a love note once in a while, or take her out on a date. Sixth, a man should never be alone with another woman other than his wife. A husband should never discuss his wife with another woman. Seventh, the man should be transparent and honest so that there are no secrets to hide from her. Your wife should know all of your passwords, know where you put the keys to your car, know how much is in your joint bank account, and know, if she asks, where you've been all day (unless it's a surprise for her).

To the Woman

The first need of a man is to have sexual satisfaction. This is without question. Second, the woman should esteem and respect her husband by listening when he speaks, and not contradict him in the presence of others – don't crush his ego. Third, infidelity is not just a male sin. As a pastor and counselor for over 25 years, my heart breaks when I listen to stories like, "My husband was emotionally unavailable to me, so I met someone else who could fill that need." Breaking the marriage covenant is an egregious sin. Fourth, don't discuss your husband with other men. When you do so, you betray your vows to love, honor, and respect him. Don't speak negatively about your husband to your friends or seek counsel from them about your marital problems. Fifth, don't keep any secrets from each other because transparency and honesty are the foundations for Godly intimacy. Some of the things a woman can do to enhance the love relationship with the husband is to write him cute notes, prepare his favorite meal, wear the dress she know he likes, or purchase something small or frivolous for him, something that he wouldn't buy himself. Give him a nicely framed picture of yourself and/or your children for his office desk. Surprise him with an all-expense paid trip to do something he likes. Put the children to bed early and prepare a candle lit dinner. Do something that you recall he liked when you were dating. Take walks together in the park. Go bungee jumping. Greet him warmly when he comes home after work. Help him get the junk out of his car and/or garage. Do something to lighten his load.

Prayer

- Lord, help me to be unselfish and seek out to fulfill my mate's needs. Let me always put my spouse first in his or her sexual desires.

Tips

- Invite God's presence before and after you have sex through prayer. Complement each other after sex. Don't go to bed angry with each other. In order to consummate sex in the evening, you have to start working on it with the way you speak, touch, and relate throughout the day.

Reflections on your Sex Life

- Write down your definition of sex.
- Do you follow the Designers pattern of sex, or the cultural sex pattern?
- What's your plan to fight sexual temptation?
- What grade, A-F, would you give yourself in intimacy – sexually, emotionally, and spiritually – in your marriage?
- What plans do you have to improve your sex life in the areas above?

CHAPTER 7

Building a Winning Team: The win-Win-win Paradigm for Solving Conflicts in Marriage

"Be careful that when you get on each other's nerves, you don't snap at each other. Look for the best in each other and always do your best to bring it out."

(1 THESSALONIANS 5:15 MSG)

Dispelling four Myths in Marriage

1. Mr. & Mrs. Right

There is no Mr. or Mrs. Right out there. If you are looking for Mr. Right or Ms. Right, you are chasing after an illusion. Instead, decide to become the right person God created you to be. One of the characteristics of an others-oriented person is being a generous giver. They allow others to be real in their God-given pursuit as they develop the characteristics that God commands. Writing to the Philippians, Paul said, "Let nothing be done through selfish ambition or conceit, but in lowliness of mind let each esteem others better than himself. Let each of you look out not only for their own interest, but also for the interest of others. Let this mind be in you which was also in Christ Jesus."[1]

2. The Perfect Marriage

There are no perfect marriages because two individuals are imperfect in and of themselves. Some unmarried people believe that there are conflict-free marriages. That is a myth. Every marriage has challenges in their relationship. For some marriages, the conflict might be as minor as disagreeing on where to squeeze the toothpaste. In others, it gets as serious as physical or emotional abuse.

3. Marriage causes Problems

Some people say marriage creates or causes conflicts. This is erroneous and nothing could be further from the truth. Someone once said, "Marriage doesn't create conflict, it only **reveals** our selfish nature."

4. Marriage brings Happiness

Lasting happiness is not found with people, events, or activities. Genuine and true happiness is found in one Person—The Lord Jesus Christ. So put your trust in the One who created joy and happiness.

The Difference between Conflict Resolution and Reconciliation

There is a big difference between these two words: resolution and reconciliation. In a marriage conflict, our focus should be on reconciliation rather than resolution. Reconciliation only seeks to reestablish the relationship, whereas resolution seeks to resolve every single issue in a marriage. The reason why a resolution is probably not going to work is that couples don't always agree on the same things. In reconciliation you strive to work out the differences on major things that you disagree on. We want to be bridge builders not wall builders.

Let's be clear. Conflict is unavoidable in any human relationship, but it can also be healthy in marriage. If the husband and wife are given biblical tools to assist them in reconciling their differences, their marriage will be healthy. It must be said that all thriving marriages have one thing in common: they always work out their problems. We will introduce the win-Win-win model to solve most of our marital troubles, but first we must examine the root of the conflict.

Even in a great relationship, there will be disagreements, so the couple needs to fight fair. Healthy relationships aren't conflict free; they ought to be conflict solving. Couples nowadays fight for victories rather than solutions. When we fight for victory, the result is that one party wins and the other loses. Part of the problem is also that God isn't brought into the equation of the conflict. This chapter will focus on outlining some of the win-Win-win strategies to help every couple fight the good fight and emerge as winners. Paul says that he's fought "the good fight". Couples too can fight the good fight and have a healthy relationship.[2]

The Source

In order to solve any of life's challenging problems, the best route to take is to trace the problem from its source. The cause of all conflict in human relationships does not come from people who wish you ill, nor from our distressing circumstances, nor from Satan or demons. It is primarily rooted in our narcissistic personalities, which are deeply rooted in our sin nature. A secondary source that impedes human relationships is having unrealistic expectations of others. Pride is the third source, at the heart of the human conflict.

First, Jesus says that our problems don't come from without, but from within: "And He said, 'What comes out of a man is that which defiles a man. For from within, out of the heart of men, proceed evil thoughts, adulteries, fornications, murders, thefts, covetousness, wickedness, deceit, lewdness, an evil eye, blasphemy, pride, and foolishness. All these evil things come from within and defile a man'."[3] Likewise, the apostle James poses a couple of questions which lead us to discover the source of our conflicts. He writes, "What is causing the quarrels and fights among you? Isn't it the whole army of evil desires that war within you? You lust and do not have. You murder and covet and cannot obtain. You fight and war. Yet you do not have because you do not ask. You ask and do not receive, but you ask amiss, that you may spend it on your pleasures."[4] The couple's greatest problem is narcissism, or self-centeredness. It stems from "self" and manifests itself in various forms: selfishness, self-righteousness, self-sufficiency, the 'me-myself-and-I' syndrome, self-absorption, self-deception, and self-gratification, just to mention these. The root of self is found in pride. The antidote for self is to be Christ-centered and others-focused. Having a Christ-centered lifestyle means that the couple submits and depends totally on the Holy Spirit to control their lives while they serve each other and those in their immediate sphere. As they submit to the Holy Spirit, God will gradually chip away their character flaws: gossiping, lying, cheating, manipulating, deceiving, withholding forgiveness, and grudges.

Second is the problem of having unrealistic expectations of others. When we make demands that others can't meet, it causes frustration and even leads to resentment and bitterness. The good news: relational problems have a cure. The remedy is God's love. The apostle John writes, "Now dear friends, let us continue to love one another, for love comes from God. Anyone who loves is a child of God and knows God."[5] God's love is unconditional, eternal, sacrificial, and others-focused. The other bigger news is that God has poured His love in each believer through the Holy Spirit,[6] so we as believers have no excuse for not loving as God loves. God says, "I will show you my love forever, so says the Lord who saves you."[7] Through Isaiah, God is telling us that His love is unchanging, steadfast, irresistible, and undying. Therefore, Jesus gives us this instruction, "I command you to love each other in the same way that I love you."[8] Peter echoes Jesus' sentiments in the text verse above, where he enjoins us to love others because our love will cover all offenses against us.

Third, pride is at the heart of conflict. We refuse to submit to one another. Solomon quips, "Only by pride comes conflict."[9] For example, yeast is a classic metaphor for pride and arrogance. When one puts yeast in dough it puffs up. A little yeast (pride) blows things out of proportion so that whenever you find yourself in a conflict, pride is at the very root of it. Pride says in a conflict, "I am better", "I am superior", and "I know more than you". Whereas humility says, "I value you", "I prefer you more than myself", "I appreciate you more", and "I'm willing to learn from you". As said earlier, healthy marriages thrive best when couples practice submission and service to one another. Jesus said it best, "So in everything, do to others what you would have them do to you..."[10] As Scripture reveals, Jesus paid the ultimate price when He took upon Himself the form of a servant and was made into the likeness of man and being found in fashion as a man, He humbled Himself and became obedient onto death, even the death on the cross.[11]

Inspired by the Holy Spirit, Paul outlines four daily habits to maintain lasting, healthy relationships. He declares, "Love never stops being patient, never stops believing, never stops hoping, never gives up."[12] The first secret to lasting love is extending grace to those who offend us – love never stops being patient. We extend the same forgiveness, mercy, and grace to others as God does to us every day. Second, we must express faith in the people we relate to. We cannot say we love people when we don't believe in them, because faith and love are interwoven. Love never stops believing. Third, love never stops hoping. We must always expect the best out of others. Recalling, rehearsing, and rehashing past failures is unhealthy and unproductive. Delete them from your mind. Finally, lasting love never gives up. It endures through every circumstance and always perseveres; it never looks back; it keeps going until the end. Love is a learned habit. It takes intentionality and practice. It is something you can get good at, and that means you can only get better at loving others by practicing love. "Practice these things; be committed to them, so that your progress may be evidence to all."[13] Pride is also at the heart of conflict when we refuse to submit to one another. "Only by pride comes conflict."[14] An attitude of pride is self-confidence, such is a person who is full of themselves and believes they are superior. Arrogance on the other hand is an attitude of insecurity where an individual uses the insecurity to cover up their sloppiness and inability to cope with a task. People with such attitudes are very defensive and end up being very frustrated. Referring to our classic metaphor of yeast, when yeast is put in dough it puffs it up. So a little yeast (pride) blows situations out of proportion and whenever you find yourself in a conflict or argument, pride is manifested.

win-Win-win Strategies on Handling Conflicts

A wise man once observed, "All human conflicts are based upon differing expectations." If you think about it, it has some element of truth. You get married expecting one thing; your spouse expects something else. You get home in the evening, you picture putting your feet up, but your spouse has a honey-do-list waiting for you. In all of life, not just marriage, our differing expectations pave the way for disappointment and conflict. Because men are wired differently than women, differences are inevitable in the home. Moreover, individuals have different temperaments because they come from different family backgrounds, bringing with them different traditions, habits, and thought patterns into the marriage.

The secret to a healthy, thriving relationship is learning how to fight fair using the win-Win-win strategy. What is the win-Win-win strategy? This method recognizes, first and foremost, that God should be at the center of the relationship. The middle Win represents God and His word and beside it are the husband and wife. Whenever conflicts or disagreements arise at home, the couple is inclined to be self-focused during these moments. Each party presents logical arguments that favor their perspectives and discredit the position held by their partners. This tendency in men and women goes back to Genesis when God told Adam, after the fall, that he had dominion over his wife. Due to our inherent fallen-ness, self-conceitedness, and self-righteousness, couples are incapable of settling their conflicts judiciously. Thus, they need a third and unbiased party to bring sanity and resolution into their problem. When they turn to God and His Word during their fights, God's counsel will make both of them come out as winners. As a counselor with over 25 years of experience, the win-Win-win paradigm has always worked. The few cases where the strategy wasn't successful were when the couple ignored God's word.

Our overarching goal in this book is to work at oneness and intimacy in marriage. Here are eight practical examples for handling conflicts:

1. Make the first move

As a peace maker and a bridge builder, take the initial step to resolve your problem. Jesus said, "So if you are presenting a sacrifice at the altar in the Temple and you suddenly remember that someone has something against you, leave your sacrifice there at the altar. Go and be reconciled to that person. Then come and offer your sacrifice to God."[15] God does not accept the gifts of either partner if their problems are not settled. Reconciliation is an intentional act and the only way to solve the conflict is to face it head on. The challenge that most people have is fear. The couple may be afraid to take the initial step because they don't want to be vulnerable or rejected, or they want to be in control of the situation. However, Scripture admonishes us that we have *not* been given the spirit of fear but of power, love and sound mind.[16] Our love must exceed our fears. The Bible weighs in and lets us know that perfect love casts out fear.[17] Remember, God blesses those who are peacemakers for they will be called the children of God. By taking the first step towards solving your problem, you're demonstrating that you are a peacemaker and bridge builder. For husbands, it is crucial to remember that you take this step because your prayers are hindered if your wife is angry with you. Conflicts block your fellowship with God. Here are five suggestions to consider when meeting with your spouse:

- Pray for the details of the meeting.
- Chose the right time for both parties.
- Choose the right place.
- Come with a positive attitude.
- Establish some ground rules. For example, both parties should agree that certain words are out of bounds (i.e. divorce). Instead, declare intentionally that the marriage will work. Avoid using harmful and destructive words.

2. Ask God for Wisdom

Intentionally plan a peace conference between you and your spouse. Pray that God will give you wisdom on the important issues you want to resolve. "If you want to know what God wants you to do, ask him, and He will gladly tell you."[18]

3. The actual peace conference

Begin by owning up to your own fault. Confess your wrongdoing to your spouse. Don't make excuses for yourself, attack your mate, or defend yourself, but look introspectively to your faults. Earlier, the apostle James informed us that fights and quarrels come from within us. When a partner has inner peace, what happens outside does not upset them, but when we don't have inner peace the converse is true. Our modern day lawyers have coined words and phrases such as "incompatibility" and "irreconcilable differences" as reasons for couples to break up. This concept is unbiblical because the primary purpose of marriage is not to make you happy but to make you holy like Jesus. You can learn to love anybody because love is a choice and it is always more rewarding to resolve a conflict than to dissolve a relationship. At this peace conference, try to avoid getting your feelings hurt. It demonstrates pride and arrogance instead of humility and maturity. Solomon says, "Pride only leads to arguments...."[19] Sometimes you need to say, "I'm sorry, I was only thinking of myself." This statement will break any deadlock in a relationship. Come to the conflict table with a humble heart. Jesus said, "Why do you notice the little piece of dust in your friends eye, but you don't notice the big piece of wood in your own eye. First, take the wood out of your own eye then you will see clearly to take the dust out of your friend's eye."[20] The great principle here is you need to confess your part first.

4. Now listen to your partners hurt and perspective

Generally, couples tend to argue over ideas, but the point of primary importance is our feelings and emotions. People who are hurting hurt others, but people who are at peace give peace to others. Similarly, people who are loving give love, but those who are hurt inside can only give others their pain. So, if you want to help others, start with listening to their needs, their hurts, their concerns, and their interests. So, "...be quick to listen, slow to speak, and slow to get angry."[21] Training ourselves to be good listeners is the key to diffusing conflicts. As a rule of thumb, always listen before you speak. We will elaborate on this concept later in greater detail. Couples also ought to train themselves to look out for the interests of others instead of themselves. Paul states, "Each of you should look, not only to your own interest, but also to the interest of others. Your attitude should be the same as that of Christ Jesus."[22] You ought to intentionally shift your focus from self to others. You are more like Jesus when you focus on others rather than on yourself. While on the cross, Jesus focused on us, not Himself. Let the initiator of the conference seek to understand before seeking to be understood. Couples are commanded to be patient when dealing with each other. Paul says, "...We must be considerate of the doubts and fears of others...."[23] Let's please our partners not ourselves and do what is for his/her good and thus build them up in the Lord. All fears are irrational because fear is just false evidence appearing real.

5. *Tactfully speak the truth in love*

One is never persuasive when they are abrasive. However, if we speak the truth tactfully, kindly, gently, and reasonably, the hearer receives what we say. "Reckless words appear as a sword, but the tongue of the wise brings healing."[24] You never get your point across by being cross. Always remember that trust without love brings resistance, but trust with love brings reception. Listen to what Paul says, "Do not use harmful words, but only helpful words. The kind that builds up and provides what is needed."[25]

6. *Fix the problem, don't play the blame game*

Always try to focus on the issues and not on each other. Remember that both of you are on the same team and not opponents. When you blame each other, you are not fixing the problem. The Bible says that we should rid ourselves of this attitude. "But now you must also rid yourselves of all such things as these: anger, rage, malice, slander, and filthy language from your lips."[26]

7. *Focus on reconciliation not resolution*

As earlier said, reconciliation strives to achieve re-establishment of the relationship or "to bury the hatchet". In other words, the couple is determined to no longer hold grudges. On the contrary, resolution seeks to resolve every aspect of the conflict, which is impossible. The couple should be committed to building bridges rather than building walls. We live in a broken world — broken lives, broken families, broken relationships, and broken treaties. Strive to always bring peace between the two parties in a relationship. As Christians, we should remember that God calls us to be ambassadors of reconciliation. Paul, writing to the Corinthians said, "God has restored our relationship with Himself through Christ and has given us this ministry of restoring relationships. God was in Christ restoring his relationship with humanity... He didn't hold people's faults against them, and He has given us this message of restored relationships to tell others. We are Christ representatives...we beg you on behalf of Christ to become reunited with God."[27] God is never mad at us, He is mad about us. Every couple should strive to be imitators of God since we are God's children. God has done everything to put us back in fellowship with Him. He paid the sin debt through Christ. God has promised to bless those who make peace. Being peacemakers demonstrates that we are children of God.

8. Focus on listening more and speaking less

Adrian Rodgers once said in his radio broadcast, "Some folks don't do a good job of settling their conflicts. Rather than being married by the justice of peace, I believe they were married by the secretary of war." Under the inspiration of the Holy Spirit, James penned these words, "So then, my beloved brethren, let every man be swift to hear, slow to speak, slow to wrath; for the wrath of man does not produce the righteousness of God."[28] This passage outlines three powerful guidelines for solving conflict in the relationship.

- **Be swift to hear:** Couples and individuals need to cultivate the art of listening more than speaking even though we all have the tendency to speak more. Listening doesn't come naturally, so we have to train ourselves to understand what the other person is saying. With determination and commitment, we can all become good listeners. We gain two huge benefits from the relationship when we listen to our spouse. Our spouse believes that we love and value them when we give them our undivided attention. Hence, we encourage them to talk and open up to us. When you listen, you don't only hear their words, but you hear their heart, something that is even more important. You listen to understand their pain or joy by being a good listener. In this process, you will achieve the goal of oneness, intimacy, and closeness. Here we deal with our narcissistic problem by not letting our egos raise their ugly heads. When we assume that we understand what our mate is saying, we are not really hearing what they *are* saying. Do you know why God gave you two ears and one mouth? Listen twice as much as you speak. How should we listen? With observation. Don't look away from someone who is talking to you. It is an uncomfortable experience to have someone whose eyes are focused elsewhere when you are speaking to him or her. Listening entails looking at a person with your eyes AND ears. Even in the heat of an argument, look into your spouse's eyes tenderly. If you turn and look the other way, they have the right to assume that you don't care. A person's body language and facial expression will tell you much about the dialogue. By looking into their eyes, you observe joy or fear and anger or confusion, so listen by observation. Lean in a forward posture to show your mate that you're interested in what they're saying. Listen not only with your eyes and ears, but with your mind as well. Avoid listening when you're **hungry**, **angry**, lonely, or **tired** (HALT). You should be in a relaxed, content mood. Even under the best conditions, psychologists tell us that we can retain about 25% of what we've heard. We must cultivate an attitude of focused, concentrated effort to listen. In addition, we should listen with consideration. Don't prejudge your mate, assuming that you know what they are about to say. Instead, endeavor to discern the meaning of their words. To achieve clarity, allow your mate to express himself or herself fully without interrupting them. Once they've finished, ask their permission to say something, and then try to restate what they've said for greater understanding. Ask if you've done a good job. If you've misunderstood them, they have a chance to correct you. There are times when we think we heard what was said, when indeed our spouse denies that they said what you think they said. So, clarifying what they are communicating to you is essential in being swift to hear.

- **Be slow to speak:** Again, James reminds us to be swift to hear, slow to speak. Many times in life, my words have gotten me into trouble. I either misspoke, embellished, or outright misrepresented what I heard. Even though our ears are placed on the sides of our head, God deliberately put our tongues inside of our mouth to guard it. To avoid saying words that are not edifying, Scripture provides eight prescriptions.

1. "In a multitude of words, sin is not lacking, but he who restrains his lips is wise."[29]

2. "A soft answer turns away wrath (anger), but harsh words stir up anger."[30]

3. "The tongue of the wise uses knowledge rightly, but the mouth of fools pours forth foolishness."[31]

4. "A wholesome tongue is a tree of life, but perverseness in it breaks the spirit."[32]

5. "He who has knowledge spares his words, and a man of understanding is of a calm spirit."[33]

6. "Even a fool is counted wise when he holds his peace; when he shuts his lips, he's considered perceptive."[34]

7. "Do not be rash with your mouth or let your heart utter anything hastily before God. For God is in Heaven, and you are on Earth, so let your words be few."[35]

8. "...a fool's voice is known by his many words."[36]

From these Scriptures, we learn very endearing lessons. Do not talk too much. It's hard to talk and listen at the same time. When we are not listening, we are not learning. Paul admonishes us when he writes to the Ephesians, "Let no corrupt word proceed out of your mouth, but what is good, for necessary edification, that it may impart grace to the hearers."[37] Similarly, in his letter to the Colossians, Paul instructs the brethren: "Let your speech always be with grace, seasoned with salt, that you may know how you ought to answer each one."[38] It is significant to notice from these verses that we must be determined to cultivate words that are graceful, wholesome, and that gladden the heart. We must work hard at avoiding corrupt words that don't edify.

- Be slow to anger: James further says, "...for the wrath of man does not produce the righteousness of God."[39] The amplified version gives this rendering to the verse: "...slow to take offense and to get angry." If you have an uncontrolled temper or if you are given to temper tantrums, hear what God says to your relationship, "You are only hurting yourself with your anger."[40] and in the NKJV, it says, "You who tear yourself in anger." "An angry man stirs up strife, and a furious man abounds in transgression."[41] God is saying that anyone who cannot rule his spirit has a weak character. If we don't learn to control our anger then tragedy is bound to come our way and it might wreak havoc in our marriages and in other areas of our lives. Anger is a natural emotion given to us by God, but when we allow it to control us we experience devastating consequences. The Bible warns, "Be angry and do not sin, do not let the sun go down on your wrath nor give place to the devil."[42] Clearly, when you dwell on your anger, you invite the Devil to come in and destroy your relationship. To effectively deal with anger, use this timeless principle, the four R's:

Resolve

Determine to manage it. "A fool gives full vent to his anger, but a wise man keeps himself under control."[43] In other words, determine beforehand that no matter what happens to you today, you will not let your anger take the better part of you. After all, anger is a choice we make. A good example is when you're mad with your spouse and your phone rings. You change your tone fast as you switch gears from arguing with them to picking up the phone and responding with a calm, measured voice.

Remember

Remember the cost. Scripture gives us a variety of warnings about having a hot temper. "A hot tempered man... gets into all kinds of trouble."[44] "Hot tempers cause arguments."[45] Anger causes mistakes. "People with hot tempers do foolish things."[46] "The fool who provokes his family to anger and resentment will finally have nothing worthwhile left."[47]

Reflect

Reflect before reacting. We need to think before speaking because, "A stupid man gives free reign to his anger; a wise man waits and lets it grow cold."[48] "A man's wisdom gives him patience."[49] Always delay saying anything brash at a pivotal point, because when things are expressed in the heat of the moment it's hard to retract them. During a time of reflection, ask yourself these questions, "Why am I angry",

"What did they really say?", "Have I put enough thought into what I'm going to say next?" Then say this prayer with the Psalmist, "Lord, help me control my tongue; help me be careful about what I say."[50]

Release

Release your anger appropriately. The wrong way includes, "I'm going to give them a piece of my mind." Instead, use this Biblical approach: *Express it* – Speak the truth in love. This resolves conflicts, while strengthening relationships. Don't attack your spouse by name calling. For example, if your wife or husband is always late to events, you can ask them, "Is my time valuable to you?"

Don't use the following approaches:

- *Suppress it* – In this case, all you're really doing is bottling up your anger and putting more pressure on yourself. You appease others by suppressing it, hoping to have peace in the home. This could lead you to momentary peace, but will later haunt you and lead your marriage to serious trouble. Because one of these days, keeping it all inside will backfire, and if that anger bursts into flames, it could engulf your home. If someone gets violent and the other gets silent, you're headed for trouble.

- *Repress it* – When you are in denial, you're acting like nothing's wrong, hoping the problem will just go away. This only leads to depression. Depression can cause spiritual, emotional, and physical damage to your health and your relationship.

Taming Your Tongue – Two Practical Steps

Anger is first and foremost a product of your mind. The Bible says, "Your thoughts control your life", and "all temptations happen in the mind."[51] Your mind is your greatest asset, so Satan constantly targets it. Once you learn how to think Biblically, you can develop new attitudes which will in turn affect the way you speak and act. As we renew our minds, we learn new habits that will help us communicate with grace to our spouses. Husbands are admonished by the Scriptures to love their wives and not to treat them harshly. Peter warns that a husband's prayer will be hindered if his wife is angry with him.

A word of caution to the unmarried: don't be engaged to a man or woman who's hot tempered. Don't think you'll change them when you're married. "Keep away from angry, short tempered people, or you will learn to be like them...."[52]

The second aspect is to always rely on the power of the Holy Spirit within you to help pacify your anger. The Bible says, "Patience and encouragement come from God. I pray God will help you agree with each other the way Jesus wants."[53] Since you've received a new heart[54] you have to practice cleansing it daily, and you don't have to do it alone because the Holy Spirit is there to help you. I can testify to the fact that as my wife and I have followed these principles for 35+ years, we've drawn closer and more intimate to each other than ever before. Our children and friends who visit our home can testify that we have a loving home and are happily married. We experience God's grace daily as we submit to the Holy Spirit to work things out for us. In his radio program, Adrian Rodgers once said, "Everyone needs three homes: a family, a church home, and a heavenly home, and Jesus is the key to all three."

Quick Questions: Have you given your heart to Jesus? Are you saved from your sins, the Devil, and Hell? Are you sure Jesus lives in your heart? If you do not know Jesus Christ as your personal Lord and Savior, receive Him today. If this is what you desire, say this prayer from your heart:

Prayer

- "Lord Jesus, forgive me of my sins, come into my heart and be Lord of my life." Amen
- Lord, I echo David's prayer when he said "I am determined not to sin in what I say." [55]
- Let's also repeat what he said: "Let the words of my mouth and the meditation of my heart be acceptable in your sight, O Lord, my strength and my Redeemer."[56]

Tips to Resolve Conflicts

- Avoid the blame game. Avoid phrases like "you always" "you never" and "it's your fault." Instead, use phrases like "I feel" "I need" or "It seems to me".

- Avoid accusatory language like "I told you so", "You're always in a bad mood", "You're never satisfied", "There's nothing I can do to please you", "All you do is complain", "Why do you think you're always right?", "You're just like your father/mother", "You don't think before you speak", "It's all your fault", "You're getting what you deserved", "When are you going to be responsible around here?", "I can't imagine that I'm putting up with you", "You're so full of yourself", "That's stupid", "That doesn't make sense", "You deserve a dose of your own medicine."

- Never give your spouse an ultimatum or make a veiled threat like: "If you do that one more time, I don't know how long we'll last". Do not compare your spouse with other men or women. Don't be preachy to your spouse. Ask the Lord to show you what you need to work on in this area.

- For Diffusing Anger: Avoid talking about hot issues before meals or bed time.

- Key – Look for a suitable time to bring up contentious issues. Remember to be slow to anger.[57] "Fools show their arrogance at once, but the prudent overlook an insult."[58] David got it right when he said, "I will guard my ways, lest I sin with my tongue; I will restrain my mouth with a muscle..."[59] It's forbidden to criticize your spouse in public or private.

- Practice grace when you're dealing with your spouse because you're both a work in progress.
- Be willing to accept one another in the good times and the bad.
- "Be subject to one another:"[60] Mutual submission to one another is the key to a happy marriage. We do this by learning to adjust to each other's needs, desires, goals, dreams, and quirks.
- Be willing to change; know that you can't change anybody but yourself. Finally, "Keep your tongue from evil, and your lips from speaking deceit. Depart from evil and do good; seek peace and pursue it."[61]
- In sum, note that all great marriages are characterized by two great forgivers.

Reflections on how to be a Winning team

Discuss four Biblical ways to control your anger.

How can you tame your tongue?

What one thing characterizes all great marriages?

SCRIPTURE VERSES CITED IN THIS BOOK

GN–Good News Bible
New York: American Bible Society (1966)

GWT–God's Word Translation
Grand Rapids: World Publishing, Inc. (1979)

HCSB–Holman Christian Standard Bible
Nashville, TN: Holman Bible Publishers (2004)

LB–Living Bible
Wheaton, IL: Tyndale House Publishers (1979)

NCV–New Century Version
Dallas: Word Bibles (1991)

NEB–New English Bible
Oxford and Cambridge University Press (1970)

NIV–New International Version
Colorado Springs: Biblica, Inc. (1978-1984)

NLT–New Living Translation
Wheaton, IL: Tyndale House Publishers (1996)

MSG–The Message
Colorado Springs: Navpress (1993)

TEV–Today's English Version
New York: American Bible Society (1992)

NOTES

Introduction

The Creation of the Universe

1. Hebrews 1:3
2. Psalm 102:25
3. Genesis 2:18
4. Genesis 1:1
5. Hebrews 2:7
6. Philippians 2:5-7
7. Philippians 2:9-10
8. Genesis 2:7
9. Genesis 1:26-27
10. Genesis 2:21-23
11. John 10:10
12. Psalm 11:3

Is God your Father

1. Jeremiah 29:11
2. Ephesians 1:5
3. Romans 5:12
4. Psalm 51:5
5. Ezekiel 28:15
6. 2 Corinthians 4:4
7. 2 Corinthians 11:14
8. Ephesians 2:2
9. 2 Thessalonians 2:9
10. Revelation 12:9; 20:2
11. John 8:44
12. 1 John 5:19
13. Galatians 3:13
14. Romans 8:17
15. Jeremiah 29:11
16. 1 John 1:8-9
17. Romans 8:29
18. Matthew 28:20b

Chapter 1

1. 1 Corinthians 11:11 (LB)
2. Malachi 2:14
3. Genesis 2:18
4. Matthew 19:6
5. (Harmmcaldwell.com/2 015/02/17/cohabitation/ affect-rate-divorce)
6. 2 Corinthians 6:14-16
7. Deuteronomy 7:3
8. 2 Corinthians 6:14
9. Romans 1:12
10. Amos 3:3
11. 1 Corinthians 7:39
12. Ephesians 2:10
13. 1 Peter 4:10
14. Hebrews 3:1
15. Proverbs 22:24
16. Proverbs 23:20
17. Hebrew 12:15
18. Proverbs 28:25
19. Proverbs 18:1
20. Proverbs 23:6
21. Proverbs 11:25
22. Proverbs 11:17
23. 2 Thessalonians 3:10
24. Proverbs 12:24
25. Psalm 101:2
26. Proverbs 20:7
27. Proverbs 28:23

Chapter 2

1. Ecclesiastes 4:12
2. http://www.nytimes/19 87/08/11science/long- married-couples-do-

look-alike-studyfinds.html

3. Psalm 127:1
4. Genesis 2:18
5. Psalm 89:34
6. Hebrews 7:22
7. Hebrews 9:16-18
8. 2 Corinthians 5:14-15
9. Romans 6:8-11
10. 2 Corinthians 5:21
11. 1 Corinthians 11:11 LB
12. Ephesians 5:21
13. Proverbs 27:17
14. Matthew 19:5-6
15. Philippians 4:13
16. Matthew 6:33
17. Psalm 51:5
18. Job 14:4
19. James 4:1
20. 2 Corinthians 9:15
21. Ephesians 4:32
22. John 13:5
23. Romans 5:8
24. Ephesians 5:32

Chapter 3

1. Pope Benedict XVI, Jesus of Nazareth (Garden City, NY: DoubleDay) 2007, 282, Charles Swindoll, Apply Grace in Marriage (Insight For Living, Publishing House Frisco, Texas)
2. Proverbs 18:22
3. James 1:17
4. Matthew 6:21
5. Psalm 139:14
6. Psalm 71:6
7. Exodus 19:5
8. 1 Samuel 16:7

9. Rick Warren, The Purpose Driven Life (Zondervan, 1st Edition, October 8, 2002) 26-27
10. Romans 5:5
11. Ephesians 1:18
12. Ephesians 5:21
13. Ephesians 5:1
14. 1 Corinthians 11:3
15. Ephesians 5:25
16. http://www.kansascity.com/news/special-reports/article298638/A mid-loss-in-Joplin-deep-love.html
17. 1 Timothy 5:8
18. 1 Peter 3:7
19. 1 Peter 3:7
20. Genesis 2:18
21. 1 Peter 3:1
22. William Harley – His Needs, Her Needs: Building an Affair-Proof Marriage (Revell; Rev Exp edition, February 1, 2011)
23. 1 Peter 3:8
24. Philippians 2:13
25. Hebrews 13:21

Chapter 4

1. Proverbs 18:20
2. 1Peter 3:10
3. Song of Solomon 6:9
4. Song of Solomon 5:10
5. Song of Solomon 6:4
6. Colossians 4:6
7. Song Solomon 5:16
8. Ephesians 4:29
9. Proverbs 16:23-24
10. Proverbs 15:1
11. James 1:19

12. Proverbs 15:4
13. Proverbs 15:4
14. Proverbs 15:23

10. 1 Corinthians 7:2-5
11. Song of Solomon 6:3 NASB

Chapter 5

1. Job 41:11b NLT
2. Psalm 24:1
3. Haggai 2:8
4. 1 Timothy 6:10
5. 2 Corinthians 9:9 NLT
6. Luke 6:38
7. Matthew 6:33
8. James 4:13-16
9. Deuteronomy 8:17
10. Proverbs 30:8-9 NLT
11. John 2:5
12. 1 Samuel 15:22b NIV
13. Matthew 6:19-20
14. 2 Peter 3:11
15. Luke 6:38 NLT
16. 2 Kings 4:1-7
17. Philippians 4:19 NLT
18. James 5:16
19. Ephesians 3:20 NLT
20. Hebrews 13:5 MSG

Chapter 6

1. Psalm 8:5
2. Hebrews 13:4
3. 2 Samuel 11:2-5
4. Genesis 39:12-13
5. 1 Corinthians 6:18
6. 2 Timothy 2:22
7. https://www.psychologytoday.com/blog/wired-success/201106/the-decline-fatherhood-and-the-male-identity-crisis
8. Romans 5:5b
9. Proverbs 13:10

Chapter 7

1. 2 Timothy 4:7
2. Philippians 2:3-5
3. Mark 7:20-23
4. James 4:1-3
5. 1 John 4:7 NLT Second Ed.
6. Romans 5:5
7. Isaiah 54:8 TEV
8. John 15:12 NLT
9. Proverbs 13:10a
10. Matthew 7:12
11. Philippians 2:8
12. 1 Corinthians 13:4-7 GWT
13. 1 Timothy 4:15 HCSB
14. Proverbs 13:10
15. Matthew 5:23-24
16. 2 Timothy 1:7
17. See 1John 4:18
18. Mathew 7:3, 5 NCV
19. Proverbs 13:10 NCV
20. Matthew 7:5
21. James 1:19 NLT
22. Philippians 2:4-5 NIV
23. Romans 15:2 TLB
24. Proverbs 12:18 NIV
25. Ephesians 4:29 TEV
26. Colossians 3:8 NIV
27. 2 Corinthians 5:18-20 GWT
28. James 1:19-20
29. Proverbs 10:19
30. Proverbs 15:1
31. Proverbs 15:2
32. Proverbs 15:4
33. Proverbs 17:27
34. Proverbs 17:28

35.   Ecclesiastes 5:2
36.   Ecclesiastes 5:3
37.   Ephesians 4:29
38.   Colossians 4:6
39.   James 1:20
40.   Job 18:4 GNT
41.   Proverbs 29:22
42.   Ephesians 4:26-27
43.   Proverbs 29:11 LB
44.   Proverbs 29:22 LB
45.   Proverbs 15:18 GN
46.   Proverbs 14:17 GN
47.   Proverbs 11:29 LB
48.   Proverbs 29:11

49.   Proverbs 19:11
50.   Psalm 141:3 NCV
51.   Proverbs 4:23 TEV; Romans 7:22-23 LB
52.   Proverbs 22:24
53.   Romans 15:5 NCV
54.   Ezekiel 36:26
55.   Psalm 17:3b NLT
56.   Psalm 19:14
57.   James 1:19-20
58.   Proverbs 12:16 NIV
59.   Psalm 39:1
60.   Ephesians 5:21
61.   Psalm 34:13; 1 Peter 3:10

NOTE TO THE READER

Dr. William Ekane is the founder of New Life Fellowship Global Ministries (NLFGM) and serves as senior minister of preaching and teaching at NLFGM. He and his wife organize marriage seminars across the country. He is also author of Seven Pillars of Christianity: An Introduction to the Essential Christian Doctrines. The author invites you to share your opinions to the message in this book by writing to NLFGM at 3543 Quiet Creek Ct, Marietta, GA, 30060; or you can call at 678-799-6308. You can also visit us at: nlfinternational.org

Made in the USA
Columbia, SC
13 August 2017